Do Leave out
My Right Hand —
I Am Still Alive!

Poems from the First Decade of the 21st Century

Rozi Theohari

Boston • 2010

Rozi Theohari

Do Leave Out My Right Hand — I Am Still Alive!
Poems from the First Decade of the 21st Century

Copyright © 2010 by Rozi Theohari

All rights reserved. No part of this book may be reproduced or utilized in any form or by any means, electronic or mechanical, including photocopying, recording, or by any information storage and retrieval system, without the written permission of the Author.

ISBN: 978-1-934881-46-0

Library of Congress Control Number: 2010930864

Illustration by Erla Shehu

Back cover picture by Rozi Theohari:
The Last Sunset of the old Century, 31 December 1999

Editor: Mark Chulsky

Published by M•GRAPHICS Publishing
Swampscott, MA 01907
www.mgraphics-publishing.com
info@mgraphics-publishing.com

Printed in the United States of America

To Maureen
with love and respect
from Roz Theohari
trahant 10.10.10

To My Family:
    Akil, Diana, Michael and Jan

ACKNOWLEDGEMENTS:

    Thank you, my teachers:
- Carol Baum,
- Joe Boyd,
- Kathie Gerecke,
- Karen Laing,
- Margaret Laulor,
- Maureen Lynch Edison,
- Isabell Van-Merlin

Contents

Foreword 11

Poems

Good Morning, America 13
Immigrants 14
Kindness 16
The Atlantic Avenue Shore 17
Past Participle 18
Valentine's Day 19
More than a Penny 20
Little Girl from Vietnam 21
Round 22
Dreams Are Not Black or White 23
The Husband's Leather Gloves 24
Frost's Telephone-Flower 25
Plato Seeking Eros 26
The Colors of the Trees 27
31 December 1999, 4:15 p.m. 28
One Day After One Century 29
Nahant Island 30
The Ocean 31
Yanni 32
Meditation 33
Autumn 34
In Kosova She Felt Herself Mother 35
Two Halves 36
Don't Forget My Name 37
Becoming a Grandmother 38

Invisible	39
Rhode Island, 20 February 2003	40
To Draw a Lesson	42
The Mother — Daughter Phone Call	44
The Approaching of Mars	45
Epiphany	47
To Take the Plunge	50
Ernie-the-Pastor	52
The Pope Died — long Live the Pope	53
Boston Spring	55
When Richard Gere Smiles	56
Andrew Who Resides at Saint Theresa's House	57
Observation	59
We Shall Return	60
The New England Fall	61
Rosa Parks — One Voice	62
Christmas Eve	63
Praying For a "Little Wild Daisy"	64
I Voted for Senator Edward Kennedy	65
Back to Their Ancestors	66
The Black Mona Lisa	68
Endearment	69
Five Nuns at Boston Pops	70
Blessing for Mr. Ralph Canali	71
The Mansions at Newport	72
The Last Soldier	73
The Place where I Live	74
Keeping The Light At Egg Rock Island	76
Lucky Day — 07-07-07	78
St. Mary — August 15, 2007	79
There Is a Flag in the Air	80

"For the Beauty of the Earth"	81
Amore Mio	82
The White Mulberry Tree	83
The Tennis-Player Girl	84
08.08.08 — Man And Nature: Harmony	85
The Telephone	87
"Ave Maria" into the MRI	88
To My Husband	89
The Red Hat Ladies	90
The Golden Epoch	92
The Last Prayer	93
Memorial Day Mitsubishi Sale	95
Friendship	96
09.09.09 — Lucky Number	97
They Also Faced the Sea	98
Drinking "Cobra" Beer	99
Sacrifices — Candles Doused	100
Lost	101
Con Man	102
Remembering Longfellow	103
"It Won't Be the Same"	106
"Merry Christmas Nahant"	107
The Northern Lights of 2010	109
Stopping by the Train Station on Valentine's Day	111
Visiting Amish Cemetery	112
Acting Neighborly	113
I Had a Wife	114
Unspeakable	115
Mother Teresa Descends as a Saint in 2010	116

TRANSLATIONS

I'll Tear Apart all that I Haven't Written 120
To Her 122
I Trudged on the Bridge One Night 123
He Is I 124

THE ALBANIAN LEGEND OF ROZAFAT

"Do Leave out My Right Hand – I Am Still Alive" 125

AFTERWORDS

Sense And Sensibility In The Legend Of Rozafat 151
Our Best Citizens 157

Foreword

In those far-gone childhood years, when we happily ran about, playing all sorts of games on the road going downhill towards the old college building, that much-loved cobblestone road (as most of the roads are in the town of Korce), at some point our noisy group was joined by a girl of our own age, who had just arrived in our neighborhood. She came with a shy but open smile, which never left her face. She had warm black eyes and black hair worn in tresses. She was better dressed than we, Albanian children of the 50s, with clothes that had travelled from afar, from the USA. We played together, though we did not know much about her. We only knew she was called Rozi Çeku, and that she was from the village of Dardha, with her mother, older sister, and two older brothers. We also knew about her father living far away in America. We could not know, however, how much this weighed on her heart. We did not know that she would have gladly swapped her pretty dresses with our old unseemly clothes, in order to have her father near her, of whom she heard a lot, but had never seen. I can imagine her spending hours on her balcony facing West.

Rozi did not spend more than three or four years in our neighbor-hood, and then she left the cobblestone streets of our town to go with her family to live in Tirana, the Capital city. I did not see her for a long time, though I sometimes thought of her, and her gracious smiling face. Many years later, I recognized her name, now under her new family name, Theohari, on book covers, which I read, of course, proud that my childhood friend had become a writer. But we never chanced to meet. What a wonder that we met again, after fifty years, not in Albania, but in America, in Boston, where I became the first reader of her newly-written books in the USA.

Continuing her profession as a journalist and writer, Rozi has published essays, short stories, and poetry in America as well as Albania. The stories of her books stretch over two continents, Southeastern Europe and North America. Her books focus on America as seen through the eyes of a foreigner, an immigrant. America is filtered through her heart, the image emerging through the early spiritual links of Albanians to the big country, where thousands of countrymen and women found their second home, starting more than 100 years ago. Two themes prevail in the multitude of facts and subject matters of her writings: that America is, first of all, the country of freedom and democracy secured by law, the country where labor and entrepreneurship are sublime, and second, politics, and literature, the country of George Washington and Longfellow. In this atmosphere, the Albanian community in the US has survived with its humanistic, moral, and intellectual achievements.

The Albanian world is represented by a gallery of characters belonging to different generations and professions. It begins with the early immigrants in America, who were mostly common people but also included renowned activists of the Albanian national movement, fighting for freedom from the Ottoman Empire. Rozi describes the important Albanian figures of literature and the arts who currently live in America.

The inspirational roots of these writings are surely to be found far away, some, long years ago; maybe in those years when, in our neighbor-hood, she looked yearningly from her balcony towards the West, waiting for her beloved father to come back. Others are connected to recent times, when she stands on her balcony gazing eastward towards her daughter, and ancestors. Her books are a hymn of love and longing for all Albanian immigrants.

Niko Dako
Lecturer at the Fan Noli *University, Korce, Albania*

GOOD MORNING, AMERICA

Land of Indians,
Land of Pilgrims,
Land of Americans,
Land of my dreams.
Good morning, America,
I saw you the first time and said, "Hi"
From the sky…
While I flew over the Atlantic
Tasting "Coffee Aromatic,"
I imagined the small ship "The Mayflower"
Between stormy billows
There in the ocean below.
Then I envisioned a pilgrim's cape
Puffed up by the wind,
And though covered myself, I shuddered…
But when I stepped my foot on your continent
I felt content
That I didn't receive any arrowed greeting
Instead, at the Community Minority Center,
I met Samoset,
A white-haired old Indian man
Who invited me in
Saying, "Welcome to our hearth!"
Good morning, America… Thank you!

1994

IMMIGRANTS

Two eyes
Here,
Two eyes
There,
In their homeland
Immigrants
Have not
Five senses,
But ten.
One part
Of their heart
Pours blood
Another — tears.

If you are
Close to a Cambodian
Or a Colombian,
Don't call them
Muddled!
Their bewilderment
Is real,
Because they
Live with double vision
Night and day,
Between the push and pull of feelings
To become winners of the "American Dream."
For a Vietnamese,
A skyscraper
Seems to be
A Buddhist Temple.
An Albanian imagines
A high snowy mountain.

The Sun
Is cold
For immigrants,
Would you mind

Substituting this
With
    Warm words of
        Welcome?

           1995

KINDNESS

I shook hands
With black people;
They were kind.
I met black-skinned people
For the first time in my life,
In America...

I watched happy tears
On the cheeks
Of a black woman, Dolores,
(The tears were colorless)
For the first time in my life,
In America...

I listened to words on
Black people's lips.
It seemed as if
Their grandmother
Spoke through their mouths.
I listened to words
Of black-skinned people
For the first time in my life,
In America...

I was amazed,
Seeing an old black man lying in the road
A well-dressed white gentleman —
Took off his new coat
And put it under his head
Like a pillow.
I saw... I saw...
For the first time in my life,
In America...

1995

The Atlantic Avenue Shore

On one side
ocean
moves, murmurs, whispers, sighs
in its own language.
On the other side
people
walk, murmur, whisper, sigh
in different languages.
But
the ocean and the people
understand each other.

1995

Past Participle

"Hi," Mr. Past Participle,
You have not been simple
    To know.
You walk opinionated
Anywhere you are welcomed
By modals, passives and adjectives.
You shouldn't have been so active!
    But your best friends
    Are irregular verbs
    Oh, poor students!
"Hi," Mr. Past Participle,
    A lovely tense verb:
Have you done English
Or have you been done by her?

1996

Valentine's Day

Near the window I stand,
Alone with my headache,
While I watch snowflakes — Lonesome.
All at once on the silent road,
An old couple appears
Walking on snow — noiselessly,
    When suddenly
The old man stops short,
And pulls out a red rose.
    With nobility
He gives it to the old woman.
    She embraces him.
They stay connected
    Longer than ever,
    Without moving,
    Like a monument.

. . . .

The wind dies away.
The snowdrops become
    White flowers,
And the curious, smiling Sun,
From behind a black cloud winks
Sending them a cone of heavenly light.
Sprinkling the world with
    Love's magic
Capturing me, no longer lonely
Absorbed in love's symphony.

   1997

More than a Penny

The first day, when
I came to America,
I found a penny
In the road.
   "Gold!"
I exclaimed.
(I am lucky... Ah my God!)
   We thought,
"This rich country
Is rolling in gold coins."
Today, when I see
A penny in the street,
   I think
If one feels worthless
For oneself or for society,
One is just like a penny
    Thrown down
       Carelessly...

1998

Little Girl from Vietnam

She gazes every day at the ocean
Longing for her homeland,
The freshness of spring mornings
That haunt her imagination.
She is a wise student, Khue,
Hair as black as a raven,
Yet supple and light as a feather.
When she smiles,
Her black, almond-shaped eyes
      Grow bright,
   While her voice
   Resounds sprightly.
Everyday dressed in pink
Doesn't she look pretty?
Hi, my little friend, Khue,
I pray, your smile
Will never leave
Your face.

1998

ROUND

The Sun is round,
The Moon too.
Birds fly
In circles.
Politicians
Like round tables.
 But
I am not able
 To cope
With everyday life
That turns
Attached to a pivot:
The same thing,
The same old thing
Eat food and drink,
Pay bills and taxes,
Subscriptions.
Everyday, every year
 Our society
Develops like
 A spiral.
Please, I'm tired.
I hate rotations,
I want a quiet spot.
Maybe a tomb!
 Oh, No!
Because again
I will be revolving
With the Earth
Around the Sun…
And onward.

1998

DREAMS ARE NOT BLACK OR WHITE

In the old days,
Black women
Brought up white children.
Today I,
A white girl, baby-sit
A black child,
My little, curly Cherub.
Her eyes are bright
Like May sunshine.
Her skin is soft as silk.
When she smiles
Violet roses
Flush her cheeks.
She dreams of becoming a pianist,
And I — a surgeon.
(Dreams are not black or white)
Little brown fingers close
Over my pink ones
    Creating
A butterfly with striped wings.
    By our command
    The butterfly
    Begins to fly,
And with it —
        our dreams...

1998

The Husband's Leather Gloves

Her husband died in January.
It was a terribly cold day.
Bewildered by grief,
She lost her gloves — so
She put on his leather ones.
    Amazingly,
She touched her husband's hands.
She felt the warmth and the caress
      Of his fingers!
Never again to buy new ones.

1998

Frost's Telephone-Flower

> *Dedicated to Robert Frost's poem*
> The Telephone, *1916*

When I was just as far as I could walk
From Acton — a town in Mass,
Exhausted, settled in the grass,
Move over — you hurt me!
A flower complained.
"What? — you talking?"
I am Frost's flower!
"You still exist?"
I blossom every spring,
I am why lovers
Can meet each other
More frequently and easily.
"I cannot imagine!"
You will. You do.
For now, someone is waiting for you…

1998

Plato Seeking Eros

Summer
On the beach.
He tramples
Following in
Her footprints
On soaked sand
Seeking the sentiment
The caress, the freshness
Of her skin.
In winter
She walks
In the imprint
Left by
His footsteps
In the snow
Dipping into his warmth.

Unknown to one another, there can be
Nothing else.
Nothing… until Spring…

1998

The Colors of the Trees

My grandfather left the family in 1903,
And with nine Albanian young villagers
    Immigrated to Maine.
    For five years, the ten boys
Lived and worked in the dense woods
    Without leaving.
The ten Albanian woodcutters became famous
For their skills and qualifications as lumberjacks.
They were named "The Maine's Horses."
They were wonderful at nighttime
Playing enchanting folk melodies and forest bird song imitations
On woodwind instruments of their own creation
Becoming an extension of the woods
Living together as brothers in a wood shack — they named it "konak"
Cooking their country's delicious food,
Celebrating with enthusiasm their native holidays,
Reading the future in the crosscut circles of the trees
And marking time by the leaves' hue changing.
In 1908, my grandfather and his friends
Moved to the city of Millinocket.
For the first time they saw an American city,
Where they worked at the Grenot, a paper factory.
From time to time, they visited Albania to marry and have children.
Unfortunately, in 1962 my grandfather
Became blind because of the diabetes.
He insisted on returning to Albania,
   To the village of Dardha,
Hoping that he might see again
Our family: his
Now old wife, grown children, grandchildren, and great-grandchildren
Greeted him with love and joy;
He touched our faces and named us.
He liked to sit in a chair in front of the woods.
He sighed all the time: "Maine!
Ah, you don't know how beautiful they are
The color of the trees in Maine. I can see them now!"
He was stricken and died with the words, "Maine, Maine!" on his lips,
Tears streaming from his eyes.

   1999

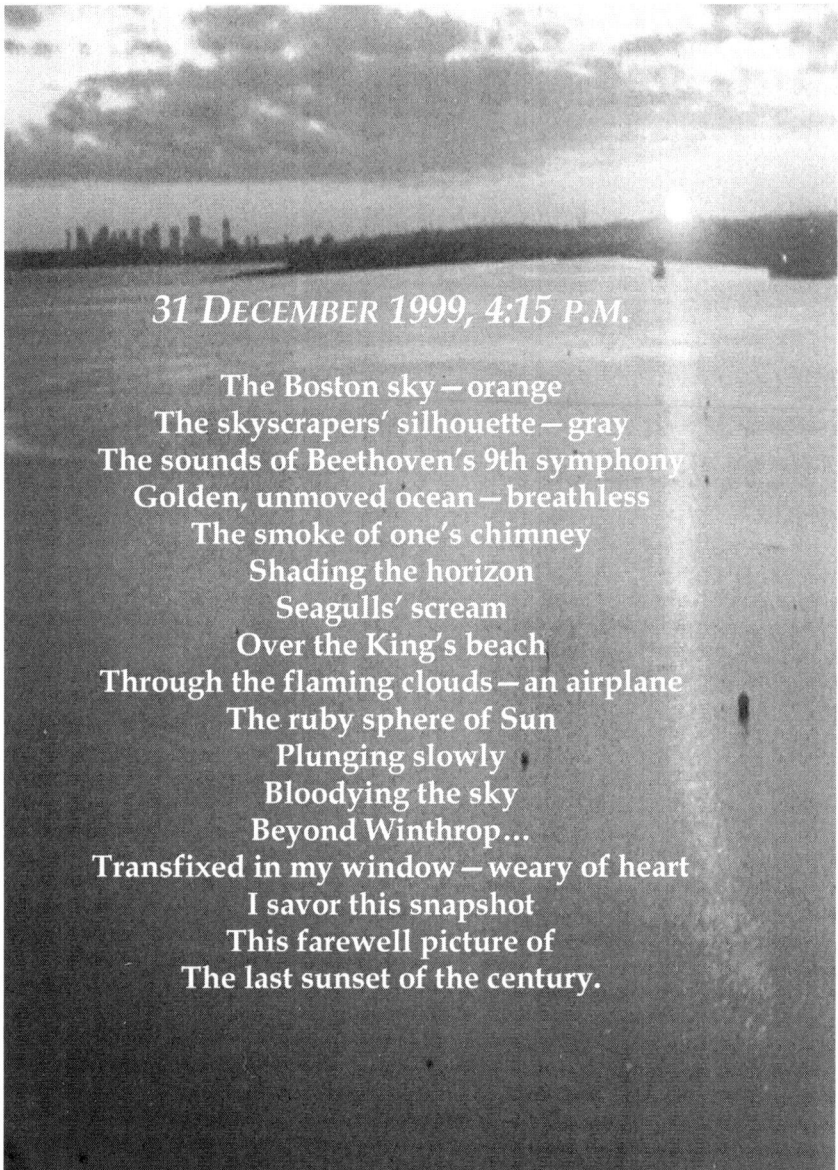

31 December 1999, 4:15 p.m.

The Boston sky — orange
The skyscrapers' silhouette — gray
The sounds of Beethoven's 9th symphony
Golden, unmoved ocean — breathless
The smoke of one's chimney
Shading the horizon
Seagulls' scream
Over the King's beach
Through the flaming clouds — an airplane
The ruby sphere of Sun
Plunging slowly
Bloodying the sky
Beyond Winthrop...
Transfixed in my window — weary of heart
I savor this snapshot
This farewell picture of
The last sunset of the century.

One Day After One Century

01.01.2000 — Good Morning, New Century!
Under the cement-frame of my balcony — hang
Long crystal icicles — like the tufts of the open curtain's scenery
Of the theater's upcoming century.

All night — the TV set gave endless scenes of the New Year celebration,
Around the globe — lights, applause, songs, cheers, champagne…
In Times Square in New York invaded by myriad people,
The ritual fiery ball climbs up…10-9-8…1 — to "2000," a bright number.
A thousand girls laughing and crying put on "2000" model sunglasses,
The dizzy planet twirls around fast with "the masque ball" dance.

At 10:00 AM — walking on the Atlantic Shore — I freeze with my camera.
The first-white-hazy sun of the 21st century
Behind me, doing the same, multilingual Boston residents
Are taking an uncompleted salutation from the sleepy Sun!
Thank you, orb, fireball, that will guide our world
For another millennium!
In my pocket the radio broadcasts the church service
From the little town of Bethlehem
Where 2000 years ago Jesus Christ was born.
Later the sounds of the traditional Vienna Concert fill the skies.
New Year 2000!
A day full of hopes, good tidings, optimism and prayers.
The world goes straight, forward and up!
And Y2K came smoothly… no problems!
01.01.2000 — I am not accustomed to writing the year!
A new hundred years — to build, restore the ruins of generations.
Oh, colors of the 21st century's face,
Please, don't repeat the tears from the years of our ancestors!
Give a chance to the Icon of Mankind
Bring "Fire" to the people —
Take a vow and commit to civilization.

2000

NAHANT ISLAND

Day time
Nahant makes the sun envious
Exposing her unbuttoned breasts.
As night falls, the sky
Embellishes her — painting lips and cheeks
With sunset's purple beams.
All night long,
She hides her face
Kissing the ocean.

2000

The Ocean

Early morning windstorm.
The surf surges, a furious gray,
Full of thick brown water
Mixed with stinking seaweeds
Onto the shore.
By afternoon the wind grows quiet.
The ocean backs off smoothly
Returning the blue view
And clear water.
But filth remains
Like the swelling chatter of gossiping women
Who turn the air blue
With nervous, uncontrollable word-storms.
How unlike angels they appear
After their
Afternoon Martini.

2000

YANNI

You stole my dream to compose your music.
Listening to those rhythms,
I return like a swallow to my nest,
To the beat of Ionian and Aegean Seas' waves dancing.
I return to the orange gardens of Greece,
To the flock with its tinkling bells
I descend, swinging through the green Pindos mountains,
On the notes of the shepherd's pipe
And the plink-plink drops of the icicles melting from Gramos rocks…
How could I know thee,
That your blessed melody
Light, as a lovely zephyr
Would bloom early in the spring
With the flowers of a familiar peach tree?
Yanni! You stole my dream.

2001

MEDITATION

And cars shall run on the street
                        as always
At nighttime the city shall wear the multicolored cloak
                        as always
And children shall laugh or cry
                        as always
And oceans shall blow or be quiet
                        as always
And people shall love or hate
                        as always
And flowers shall blossom or wither
                        as always
And Sun & Moon & Milky Way shall shine
                        as always
When I do not exist anymore.

2001

Autumn

On an Autumn day
A tree, all red
Asks me, "Hey!
Your gray hair
Painted red
Sooner or later
Will be worthless
Like my leaves
That fall today."

2001

IN KOSOVA SHE FELT HERSELF MOTHER

She is a Nahanter — Doctor Jennifer Keller —
A Dartmouth Medical School graduate.
In April 2001 she left for Pristina Hospital, Kosova,
Helping to rebuild the war-torn medical establishment.
Surprisingly, a few hours before traveling to Kosova
She was told by her doctor that she was pregnant.
After five years of marriage — the first baby!
Emotions. Exciting. Tears of joy…
Her husband's voice sounded enthusiastic over the phone.
For all that her doctor advised not to take this trip,
Jenn, a wonderful American girl, didn't change her plans.
Her husband and she could talk and think this whole thing
Through in the car on the three-hour drive to the airport.
By the time she left for Kosova
She knew she was more committed than ever
To becoming a mom.

In Pristina she felt the need to be closer to home.
Three weeks into her trip — morning sickness started;
But working in the ob/gyn clinic
She was suddenly fascinated by it all:
The pre-natal visits to the delivery of the placenta.
Kosova is having a "baby boom" after the war.
A rain of tears for the war's dead
Is replaced with babies' crying in the obstetric ward.
Doctor Keller works so fast… babies are being born
More quickly than they can be caught by midwives.
(She came from another world — as in the Indian Iroquois mythology:
"A pregnant woman fell from the sky
To multiply the human beings on Earth.")

Midnight. Jennifer is listening to the babies' hearts inside their mothers.
It seems as if these rhythms
Keep time with her own baby…
In Kosova she gave birth to herself as a mother.
She is looking forward to telling her daughter how
She spent the first six weeks of their lives together
In Kosova… Blessing all the children.

2001

Two Halves

Midnight.
Half of my bed a white shroud
Lit by a half Moon that casts a cold look at me.
I want to sleep, but can't...
A half Moon...
Its other half lights my mother's grave
Far off... in the Balkans.
Half pensive—half delirious...I cry in halves
Separated by
The dividing line of centuries.
Half despair...
Half hope... half here—half there,
We are one in the semidarkness of a half-severed Moon...

2001

Don't Forget My Name

Gently I lean my cheek on yours, my beloved.
The scent of your skin—always—linden flower.
According to our tradition, I kiss your cold right hand
As you did mine
Forty-three years ago.
Why do you stare at my face and push me away
Asking with your breaking voice:
"Who are you?"
"Your wife." My mind screams
Cursing the Parkinson's
That wreaks havoc with your memory
At your strange blue eyes—my grief pulsates, my hope cries.
Watering the garden with tears,
    The flowers know me better
I feel my empty days full of dead leaves.
Why sometimes does life's summer
End so suddenly?
While we live for remembering, drinking memory's elixir
That lengthens a spring and guides our existence.
    ...Inside, I hear you calling my name.
A voice trembling in the wilderness,
    My heart pounding.
I pick two rose roses—my name-sake you always said.
    I put one in the button-hole of your jacket,
        You open your tentative arms to me.
Well done! Please, my dearest, don't forget my name.

2001

BECOMING A GRANDMOTHER

Love is reborn in me, today,
December 10, 2001.
My sweetest dream, my annunciation brought
Good News.
I was following, like the three Wise Men,
In euphoria—to find you, my first grandchild.
Hello baby,
Welcome to this cold world.
I was waiting for you for 2000 years,
From the day Mary gave birth to her firstborn son
Watching in every blessed nursing of mother's milk,
Hearing, in every mother's voice, who sings her baby to sleep.
Hello, John, newborn,
A gift that God gave us
You, little Albanian-German boy,
I want you to be a messenger with an olive branch.

2001

INVISIBLE

      When you are going to bed, darling
      Please, don't close the window, don't.
      Fused with the night's light wind,
      I approach nearer and nearer
      Watching your rhythmic breaths,
      As I did for sixteen thousand and one nights.
There once you were my girl, my dream girl
Your face — white oleander… Falling sweetly dormant
Enumerating your twenty-five brown braids…
      My darling, don't cry.
      Your tears increase the pain
      Of our drifting apart.

      When you are sobbing at the ocean's Red Rock,
      I hover and alight near you
      Eyeing our broken love
      At the mercy of the crashing waves.
      Throwing it down on the rock's ridges
      Dissolving in enormous tears… dear
      Don't cry — I am here.

      When the Moon is up and
      Pours the gold of our love on the ocean,
      Please, my loved one,
      Make room for me in your heart
      Together to see
      And to review in delirium
Our five hundred full Moons
Sparkling forever our incandescent amour.

      When I met God and gave my life
      I said, please, send me back to my wife:
      My saint Eva… my better half,
      You are in me and I am in you; we cannot divide.

2002

RHODE ISLAND, 20 FEBRUARY 2003

As the winter is walking with white snow boots,
R.I. Spring Flower & Garden Show — Providence
Is celebrating a decade in bloom.
There where three blond girls,
Just putting in their long hair
Crowns of red tulips.
"Don't tell the tulips it's not spring."
Three girls followed by the breath of spring
Strode into the mall, where each bought
An elegant short skirt
For going dancing at a West Warwick nightclub.
Lunch time… a good time at
"Capital Grille" — right in the heart of
Downtown Providence.
Three girls with elegant figures
And red tulips in their blond hair
Ate citrus-grilled chicken sandwiches
Gazing innocent eyes
To the four round big clocks on the wall
With four different clock hands. Each clock
Named: London, Tokyo, Paris, New York.
"Different time, but they all work!
Right now in London they're dancing
Oh, what a dream — to visit those cities, some day…"
Smiled three youthful, the purest of girls.
....
The evening breezes blow the girls' hair
Walking there, to the nightclub
Where "Desert Moon"
Was rocking by Great White.
After using lipsticks and small mirrors, the three
Pushing between fans
Applauding, cheering, dancing,
Going closer and closer to the
Pyrotechnic fire
Getting burned and dying…

Their fresh tulips trampled and broken
By the running crowd…
A tragedy. A traumatic loss.
To much reality of a desert moon.
In seconds their lives' clocks stopped
Like three butterflies attracted
By the lantern's light, and getting death — A fatal attraction.
…Every winter's end
Three butterfly-girls will fly — rising and falling
Over W.Warwick, London, Tokyo, New York, Paris
Followed by the breath of spring, and dreams.

2003

TO DRAW A LESSON

Once upon a time there lived a Cadi [*]
A wise man, a powerful folk-judge of the city,
Thin, tall... very tall, a handsome man
With a nice, thick, black beard circling his face,
A beard that made other men envious.
    When he woke up every day,
The first his task was — to trim his moustache, beard and hair,
    Using small scissors.
One morning he didn't find that damn tool
And "smartly"... he lighted a candle — going
Very close — up and down the beard's whiskers
        With his right hand.
Unfortunately! In a twinkle of an eye
Half of his beard was dramatically burned.
His nerves were suddenly on edge:
        A s h a m e d.
(He would like to sink to the bottom of the sea.)

A Cadi without a beard — that cannot be!
Sorrowfully he took off his caftan-cape
    And got inside the bed
Covering... hiding his mouth and nose with the sheet.
Nervously, angrily and despairingly
He ordered his servant: "I am sick.
Nobody is allowed to see me!"

Hours passed, "the ill" Cadi
Read news and books, not leaving the bed.
   His room was such a mess!
Curiously, by chance, somewhere he read
               That
"A tall man, one time in his life
Commits a foolish mistake, but only one!"

Surprised by this, Cadi

---

[*]   *Cadi:* Ottoman official with power to judge on both civil and religious matters.

Ordered his servant again
To go to the city bazaar
"To halt" every tall man and bring them all
To the Cadi's house, into the hall.

Trembling with fear, six towering men
Stood in line at the lawgiver's door.
Cadi asked the first about his mistake
Whether anything like that happened.
"I was walking," he answered, "in a grassy meadow.
Before me appeared a cow,
I put my face between its horns,
I thought I could measure my head across
You know… the animal dragged my body…
"Stop," cried Cadi. "Next!"
Four others shared with him their stories
Of plain foolishness:
    A small catastrophe
    Or something of a joke.
The sixth, lanky man,
Terrified with anxiety,
       Accidentally
Stuck his finger between the bench's thin wooden slats.
He kept moving round and round without pulling it out
Becoming pitiful, ridiculous and scared.
"Could I please, remove him, chair and all?"
Asked the servant in a scared voice.
"Not necessary," Cadi proclaimed,
"He just proved the theory;
He made a fool of himself."

2003

The Mother — Daughter Phone Call

To my daughter for Mother's Day

— Hi, Mama, why didn't you tell me?
— Tell you what?
— Why didn't you tell me?
— A mother raises a daughter
  Teaching her confidence.
— Why didn't you tell me?
— I told you how to love and to pray to God!
— Why didn't you tell me?
— No one knows how I caressed you, girl — reciting
  In tones so sweet heart-touching stories…
— Why didn't you tell me?
— And you're still growing swiftly
  My respect for you is mingled with admiration.
— Why didn't you tell me?
— Listen, the love of a mother
  Brings blissful days, doesn't it?
— Why didn't you tell me?
— Of course my dear,
  Sometimes days are blue
  Becoming weary… very blue
  But you have a husband for praising!
— Why didn't you tell me?
— Look… you did manage your first pregnancy
  I knew you could do it — I'm proud of
  The cutest girl that a mother ever had.
— Why didn't you tell me?
— …Tell you what… my child!?
— How much I would love my baby!

May 2003

The Approaching of Mars

Hi, up there, Red Star,
Why are you watching me from the sky?
Wrapped in the mists of sleep,
Unexpectedly — I woke up.
Mesmerized by your romantic light
Saying to me, "Good morning…" Fine!
My heart went pit-a-pat
As millions of stargazers worldwide
Peered at telescopes and focused
On your — passing-planet thrills
On Wednesday — 08-27-03,
What are you telling me?

> I know something about you.
> At Boston's Museum of Science
> Years ago
> I snapped a dramatic view
> Of your small piece of rock,
> A gift from Sojourner's landing on you,
> Its size as big as a lady's ring,
> The bright grey crystals shone. Astonishing!

Welcome, Rose Planet!
During the fall, night after night, eyeing you
The way you rise and stand above my window
So lonely, so brilliant, so glorious, so fiery
And… what in the world! You followed me
To London, in front of Big Ben,
Holding my grandson in my arms
Under a moonless night sky — trying to show
Him your view with my finger
(But my baby was more attentive to my earring.
He'd really like to visit you someday.)

Hey, why did you come nearer and nearer?
Reflecting on the past...
Named by my ancestors — a Planet of the Dead
                      Giving, ill-omened
Martians, wars, violence and bloodshed
Is that a dangerous distance for Earth?
Only 34.6 million miles away?
                  Oh, wait!
Even without you presence,
Your sister Earth has
Plenty of troubles.
Is this your travel adventure?
Orbiting 60,000 years for the closest pass to us
From "Homo Neanderthal" to bring regards?

Being eyeball to eyeball with you, Mars
Amusing — the way you dance with Moon
Or count the fire-fly planes that go quickly
Making a tangent to your orange body...
Well now... enough... you godsend.
Please, descend
Here on my porch
To drink together a glass of Merlot
Or take a trip on Casino Cruise
Gambling on a boat
Navigating in Mass Bay,
Or admiring the changing color of the trees in Maine woods...
More exciting than your icy craters
In your empty body — lifeless.
Perhaps, they are not icy tears!
Did you ever see a frozen lachrymation?
Yes. But in your sister's face...

    As you do pull away from us,
    Your view is shrinking every night.
    Good Bye... Good Bye, Uncle Mars,
    Say "Hello" to our descendants
    When you are so close to sister Earth
    Again in 2287.

2003

Epiphany

      My dear grandson John,
      I know how much you love
      Watching geese flying in the sunny sky,
      But the story I want to tell
      Happened on an overcast winter day.

There is a pitiful honk in the air.
I lightly touch my face
On the window glass
The snowstorm left a blanket of fluffy white,
The white lake has turned to ice.
The dead of winter. Sixth of January!
I remember Albania's Epiphany in my small village.
Somewhere between snowy mountains
A thick, iced river
(named Jordan every sixth of January)
Faithful villagers
Singing "Jesus was baptized,"
And breaking the river's ice
In a circle large enough
For the priest to immerse the silver cross into the water.

There is a pitiful honk in the air.
Early today,
A mournful morning of misty gray
On the whiteness of the freezing lake
Near the shore
A crowd of numbed geese
That slept all night long on the glacier,
With bodies oriented to the east
As if stretched by a magnetic field
Looking like a winter sculpture.
Their claws—fixed, nailed on tight
Black hieroglyphics on the ice,
Moving only brown heads and white chins
Honking, honking and crying, crying…ing…

(Last October they didn't make
The winged migration from north to south.
An unlucky goose had its wing broken, so
They all stayed to survive the stinging cold,
The brutality of the New England winter.)

There is a pitiful honk in the air.
By a fatalist logic, in nature's history
These birds, hot-blooded beings
Couldn't resist living near the beach
In a dangerous situation in the bleak midwinter.
An iced film divided fishes underneath
From hungry, bone-chilled-cold geese up there
In the frozen air.

There is a pitiful honk in the air.
Spreading their brown and gray wings,
Geese curve their numbed shapes,
Nip the iced snow between nails and claws,
Slash their toes,
Help themselves and each other
Pat wing to wing and foot to foot,
Follow their gentle leader one by one in disorder,
Move, shake, fall, like bad ice-dancers.
Their crooked feet make noise on the ice
Like gopher's paws over yellow, dried grass.

There is a pitiful honk in the air.
My heart is crushed by pain.
A white sky — watches regretful, the same,
Looks at poor birds half dead — half alive.
…Dear Sun, we can't see you all the time,
But you observe us from afar.
The compassionate Sun — pulls out its fiery sphere
Between thick, gray clouds,
Melts ice on the lake's surface,
Creates a hole as big as a goose's body.
One by one the geese take a bath in the small puddle:
A baptism!
They discharge into the water their ache, fear, anxiety and ice.

Hopeful honks fill the air!
Vivacious geese climb on top of a black rock
Partly-covered by snow — Pandalike,
Try to expand their wings and fly without fear,
A small, gray aggregate cloud,
The airborne letter "V" — victory!
Show their white chins and bellies,
Their triumphant music-cutting sounds
Beautify the atmosphere
Flying... flying far away...
A climax, the community they belong to,
Their habitat, relationships, security, survival,
Blessed be thee... A-le-lu-ia...!

While I watch the wild geese
Disappear into the horizon,
You, John, my three-year-old grandson,
Are asleep in frigid Freiburg, Germany.
Perhaps, you dream
About the wild geese — in agony!
My Godchild, your name
Is the same:
John the Baptist,
Don't forget January sixth,
The Day of Miracles!

2004

To Take the Plunge

> *My dear grandson, Jan,*
> *on Thursday, February 12, 2004,*
> *behind our building,*
> *on the iced coast of the ocean*
> *unexpectedly, a seal appeared.*
> *At the moment I thought*
> *If you were there, with me, to see…*

Oh, you seal
The harp-shaped seal
Mottled — black and grey
Stuck on the white Lynn Harbor ice,
Like a child's drawing on paper.

"Hey, we have a visitor, there!"
She left the ocean underworld
Escaping from her caring mother
Alone in icy February, after
Traveling many miles with acrobatic
Flippers splaying… curious about the earth!
You fluffy pup — frightened and panicked
In a morning fog mixed with cold air.
                      There,
On the edge of Lynn Harbor.

Did you want the fresh air in your lungs?
Or are you hoping to meet… Whom?
Coming slowly in this gentle, peaceful place.
No noise. Only the winter silence
On 50 Lynnway, the ocean's shore.
Is it your first venture so near spring?
A long journey in the ocean
Navigating without mother's guidance,
A dangerous game?

You lift up your small head
                Directing
Your black bulging eyes

To the eight-story building's windows
Watching many grandmothers'-grandfathers' faces
In this tower for elders.
Their compassionate eyes are a message:
"To your shelter and family — go back…go back!"
Oh, you seal,
The harp-shaped seal,
Before your fate is sealed:
Do return to your mother, harp seal.
Shyly, she takes the plunge into the icy water.

2004

ERNIE-THE-PASTOR

As a hobby,
He raised prize-winning dahlias.
Ernie always won
The blue ribbon at the Baltimore flower show.
As a pastor — preaching at a nearly empty church
In the heart of Baltimore.
On the last Sunday he prayed:
"God works for good,
for those who love Him."
The very next day Ernie
Went duck-hunting on Chesapeake Bay.
Accidentally, his friend's shotgun went off
Blowing out Ernie's eyes.
Blind forever,
But still the happiest optimist
Full of joy and love and faith.
His church revived.
More families came — listened to his sermons,
Watched, hearts breaking...
He "sees" people
Who would never come to church
If he had sight.
They'd be ashamed to be recognized on the street,
A secret... with a blind man... is a secret!

Yet, the sightless pastor raises dahlias
The beautiful blooms he can never see!
He puts some of them on the altar and prays
How to begin anew,
Blessing the countless people and giving the unspoken message:
"Oh, God! Turn my heart, take my pain and my brokenness,
As you took my eyes' light
To shatter it into hundreds of pieces to light others'
Let it shine through their souls... T h a n k s!"

2004

The Pope Died — Long Live the Pope

URBI ET ORBI

1

As I remember, during
The latter part of the twentieth century
Two Roman Popes died
One right after the other.
Then, Polish Pope Wojtyła
Was elected,
In October of 1978.
When the Italians noticed
White smoke from the enclave
They whispered a complaint:
Un straniero — A foreign Pope!
For 26 years he reigned,
Father of the Earth's community.

By destiny,

A human being with his roots in prayer,
He had to fight — to change the world.
"Don't be afraid!" prayed this epic Pope.

2

Pope Wojtyła died on the 2nd of April 2005.
Three million people watched
The funeral ceremony in St.Peter's Square,
On a spring sky,
Over the Holy Father's coffin
An open Bible. The pages
Moved, facing each other
In history's wind,
To leaf through centuries,
Giving a "Follow me" — message
"God will be always with us."

3

"Long live the Pope!"
A new German Holy Father — Ratzinger,
A new path for the spiritual shepherd begins.
Un straniero!... again!
With God's help,
He'll gain the people's hearts.

2005

BOSTON SPRING

Spring is dancing over Boston
Playing a melody
With diagonal strings on the Zakim-Harp Bridge,
Accompanying the harmony
With the lilting voices of trilling birds.
Painting in pink
The myriad petals of magnolia trees.
Flying fountains of sparrows.
On the silk-royal-blue sky
Their heads set for England…
Serenity.
April's violet blue petals
Resemble a spring's blue-purple sky.
The breath of spring-spread fragrance
Indistinctly
Melds with the salty ocean air,
Envelops the lightly-dressed young girls
Adorning their romance and dreams.

Boston spring — a symphony
That leads the city
To sing with Heaven…

April 2005

WHEN RICHARD GERE SMILES

Richard Gere says:
"I cry every chance I get!"

But, when he smiles,
The red moon closes its eyes
The snow melts from Himalaya's hills
And Tibet changes its color to green...

2005

ANDREW WHO RESIDES AT SAINT THERESA'S HOUSE

— *...Wasn't then... The Cold War?*
— Yes, it was. The Berlin Wall did exist still.
  Our "USS George" — Special Force ship
  Left Greece — navigating the Ionian sea.
— *And... what did you see?*
— Your country... an Albanian city.
  It was a beautiful port.
  I made with my right hand a cross
  Then saluted: "Good morning Albania,
  Mother Teresa's birthplace!"
— *Were you a soldier there?*
— Yes, an electrician of "101 AIRBORNE DIV."
  Looking with my binoculars at your land,
  I obtained permission from my commandant;
  In minutes my boat neared the harbor.
— *Did you fear being caught?*
— You know, I believe in God!
  When your soldiers shouted: "Halt!"
  I stopped, waved my hand, smiled, prayed,
  I reached underwater and touched the sand.
  Oh..., something happened... something,
  Many sailors and civilians became rigid
  When they looked at my black skin,
  More than "an American trespasser enemy,"
  They were surprised to face an African-American.
  They never had seen one.
  That's it.
  In a blink of an eye I was back in our torpedo boat
  With a fist of moist sand,
  A memory of Teresa's land.
— *I see you here, seated in St.Theresa's House's garden,*
  Between friends, aromatic roses and chirping birds...
— After forty years from that day
  You know, I am physically weak,
  My memory is the same,

But an inner being whispers to me:
"Be blissful that you chose to live
At Theresa's apartments... downtown Lynn."
Mother Teresa's noble heart
Stays with us
In our prayer...
        forever...

> *I shook hands*
> *With the dark-skinned retired electrician,*
> *And I felt the pure current*
> *Of his white soul.*

June 2005

OBSERVATION

After the election
They didn't cut the grass
Beyond our eight-floor building on the small city's periphery,
But they cut the teacher's wages
At the Community Cultural Center,
Where he led the Poet's Club.
            Alas,
Over the city poets' verses
Now sprouts the rooting grass.

2005

WE SHALL RETURN

American flag is fluttering smoothly,
Caring and whispering the nation's injury
Of August 2005 Mississippi River flood.

Is this the Flood?
The biblical apocalypse? — Rock of Ages!
The king of water... look to thee
From "Tsunami" to "Katrina" storm ravage.
What is happening to the world's face?
Should we write again "Amazing Grace?"

New Orleans!
Take my hands
To wipe the old black ladies' tears
That echo —
The legend-Mississippi-African-American-fears.
A little American girl
Named Katrina
Changes her name to
               Hope,
And the sun will set in New Orleans.

2005

THE NEW ENGLAND FALL

The rosy Autumn returns
The ritual rhythm of the red New England,
The wild cherries, the oak forest, the maple and the beeches
Shake their red and golden beards
On mushy piles of leaves at the roots of the trees,
Combing, trimming and embellishing themselves
At the crystal-mirror lakes of Maine hills.

    The cool air is wafting a kiss
To the Fall night—waiting
For a short date with the dwindling day…

    The squirrels
Welcome each other for the Fall's dining
Using two hand-paws shelling and chewing,
Tasting
The wild chestnut with hedgehog fruit.

The Bronze Butterfly Fall Migration
Follows the journey Canada-Mexico,
The cosmic dust of her wings—secular echo
Of the sounds of the rivers—the Indians' canoes,
The ravens' caws,
The axes' wood rumble…

The ocean waves arching in wide swaths
Incandescent the green specter of
The sun's rays pecking—
Through ruined clouds tearing each other's hair…
On the seashore—foot prints of humans and dogs
Alternating—visible or not
By the shifting sand of the dunes at Cape Cod.
Under the platinum night sky, while Boston city sleeps,
At Diamond Beach
A white gull wing feather—falls and flutters in the sand
Chanting with stars.

    2005

ROSA PARKS — ONE VOICE

"Water for white"… "Water for black"
People! Mother Nature gave it for all!

    25 October 2005.
I am seated on the front seat
Of the bus from Marblehead to Boston
Reading *The Boston Globe*… At the next station
A black woman with big glasses sits near me.
She puts her brown finger
Near my pink one, on the newspaper
When she reads of Rosa Parks' death.
    We are both tearful in prayers.
In the spectrum of the woman's colorless tear
I can hear:
    " — Who are you Rosa?"
    " — A colored woman!…But
I can stop the buses!"
Never forgetting the driver's face:
    " — Are you going to move?"
    " — No!"
The "No" that brought a huge civil rights *movement*.
The "No" that *moved* America toward equality.

    * * *

"A woman sat down
And a world turned around" —
— Yet
Martin Luther King's dreams remain incomplete.

    2005

CHRISTMAS EVE

As 2005 comes to an end
Saturday, 24 December, 12:00 Noon
In broad daylight
Two jet planes in the Atlantic sky
Laying down the white puffy contrails
One, straight North-South
The other — East to West
Through Boston Bay and beyond its shores
Create a big bright, silver, vaporized cross
Fixed in the middle by a dazzling Apollo-Sungod!
The presence of the eye of the Universe...
"O come, O come Emmanuel!"
A melody echoing of angel's songs
Surrounding Boston from
Horizon to horizon.
Higher and higher the trail's prophecy cross
Stretches its wings
From Massachusetts — the free Commonwealth —
To the World.
A messenger of grace for the planet:
Truth, Hope, and Heavenly Peace on Earth.

2005

Praying For a "Little Wild Daisy"

"And now we will pray in silence!"
The Minister preached at 10:30 A.M. on Sunday,
September Third, 2006, at Nahant Village Church.
While the ladies' and men's lips moved — head-bowed,
In quietness, I invoked:
"Oh, God, why don't I find a little wild daisy
In the gardens of New England?
Back in my homeland — far... in the Balkans
Luleshqerra (the lamb-flower) — these tiny little flowers
Grow so nicely in the grass.
I remember my girlhood — daisy-ornamented crowns
Or pulling the silk petals one-by-one:
"He loves me," "He loves me not," "He loves me..."

On the very next Sunday, stepping onto the path,
I glanced breathlessly at the Nahant church's meadow,
Thousands of pineapple weeds as white as snow,
An unnoticed huge blooming of tiny wild daisies
That radiated like small spheres of Sun
Through the white petal-rays —
The sounds of the church's bell resonated
As each tiny flower — a note from the chimes
Descended from the air...

The believers with amazed faces
Asked: "Who planted this miracle in blossom?"
The church deacons raised their eyebrows.
I raised my head to the blue sky — smiling and whispering:
"Thank you God — You love me!"

   2006

I Voted for Senator Edward Kennedy

Today, Tuesday, September 19th, 2006
At the dawn of the twenty-first century
As I was going to the polls
At 10 Church Street, Lynn, Massachusetts —
Like climbing to the top of Arlington Cemetery
A rhythmic memory followed my steps:
"...Woman, don't forget... don't forget..."

    *   *   *

Three ladies — the poll workers
Checked my address — asking: "Republican?" or "Democrat?"
I took a pink Democratic ballot — the first name, "Edward Kennedy."
. . . .
A metal table, the booth and me
I blacked in the circle,
As if to fill up the unhealed bullet wounds on
The bodies of his brothers, Robert and John.
"Bullet" and "Ballot" — a fatal similarity
I voted for The Three Brothers Kennedy.

2006

BACK TO THEIR ANCESTORS

1

Let me honor Ireland,
This marvelous land
Where angels fold their wings,
Where the sounds of the streams
Whisper the poet Yeats' dreams…

Let me glorify Stone-Aged Ireland
Touching dolmens — the Cyclops stones
Walking over the basalt columns
On the Giant's Causeway.
There, through the crashing waves
Of the Atlantic sea
As long ago the giants stepped.
Visiting medieval fortresses
And many castles' roof-tops,
The green mountains, the marble caves,
The splendor of rivers and waterfalls
Full of history, myths, fairytales
Where flourishes the Celtic soul.

2

Let me congratulate
The great-grand-children of the Irish people
Who emigrated in the 1840s
From the port of Londonderry to America.
Today, in 2005, these Irish-Americans
Are sending a stone home
To connect with each other and Ireland.
There is an Irish proverb saying:
Curri mi clich er do charne
"I will add a stone to your cairn."
The engraved stones with words:
"Mother", "Bless", "Peace", "Pray…"
Are sent from America as a tribute

To the memory of "The Tonnes," a lough, where
The Foyle River meets the salty Atlantic waters
And is the legendary burial place
Of the Celtic seagod Manamman Mac Lir.
Just here, the American stones
Will be dropped into the turbulent waters
These dreams, wishes, hopes and prayers
Will sink to the Irish otherworld…

Back to their ancestors!
Homecoming:
An bealach' na bhaile!
Beyond conflict being
The post-peace message.

2006

The Black Mona Lisa

Mona Lisa at the Louvre
Flew from her frame's kingdom of five hundred years
Falling into the 21st century
To set off to Haiti, to Port-au-Prince
To meet her pretty dual identity,
The graceful Yona:
A surgeon, a swimmer, a tennis and basketball player
Thy passion, thy miracle, thy secret of cosmic beauty
Thy secret of mystery... soul's mystery... eternity...
Thy power of sincere, black, almond eyes,
Where the planets pulsate.

* * *

Mona and Yona — a moving picturesque divinity.
One is dressed in Florentine aristocratic plush,
The other, in green cotton for surgery
(Leonardo's curiosity about human anatomy)
Mona and Yona... (both French speakers now).
The white one shaded in a lace veil,
The black one with braids and sneakers.
Mona — a reader of Petrarch's sonnets,
Yona — a vessel of postmodernism.
In spite of this,
Two models of perfect feminine beauty,
White and black silk skin in light and shade silhouette
Walking intertwined between centuries in eternal calm
The Old World's queens and empresses behind them — come,
Both followed by Da Vinci — unveiling
Their enigmatic smiles
For eternity.

2006

ENDEARMENT

Driving from New York to Boston
In my beige Volvo convertible —
I leave Rhode Island behind.
The sign — "Welcome to Massachusetts"
Appears and disappears on the horizon.
I'm home... So quietly!
Far from NYC noises, colors, lights, fun...
I'm home. The New England salty wind
Beats my face.
Up — in the smiling skies — the jet planes
Draw a John Hancock's signature.
I'm home... rocks planted in the soil.
The Atlantic's music
Echoing in my soul.
My little town — my innermost calm.
Blooming wild pink cherry trees on the sidewalks,
My church bell ringing — endearing!
Getting closer to my house that knows me.
In my green garden — greeting from the garlands of roses.
My Volvo finds its place under the balcony
Where the gaze of two blue eyes have endured my absence.

2006

FIVE NUNS AT BOSTON POPS

Five nuns — girls
Not seeing left or right but only the orchestra,
As their rapt faces are pulled by "magnet" instruments
Enveloped by the *Evening at Pops.*

Five sisters wear brown habits and large black veils
With a white strip — over the forehead
Five nuns — five black statues
Seated around an empty table, like a virgin oasis
Between bare-shouldered gowned women
Who drink quietly the red, pink and white wine
Dancing in ecstasy in the arms of happy cavaliers,
The romantic idyll of Sinatra's rhythms.
Five nuns — adoring Pop music
A reminder of Whoopi Goldberg,
The black singer-actress from Chelsea, Mass.
In her movie, "Sister Act"
O Maria... Sweet seraphim... Salve Regina...

Five sisters — like five silent bodies
While listening to the music
In their warm hearts
    They see
      Jesus Christ
        As a child
          Walking barefoot...

2006

Blessing for Mr. Ralph Canali

Ralph was sixteen—doing his homework,
When his father, reading the newspaper, was disturbed:
"A boy was burned by a flaming oven.
Eighty-nine percent of his skin—charred.
Skin donations are needed from teenage volunteers."
Ralph set the pen on the table—proclaiming:
"I am the one!"
He ran to the hospital.

  *   *   *

Today Mr. Ralph—over sixty—
At The Nahant Village Church, Massachusetts,
Puts out the altar's candles after services every Sunday
Feeling the burnt boy's extinguished life
Forty seven years ago
With his failing kidneys —he couldn't survive.

—He died,
So I gave help for nothing.
And I pray for him,
And I pray for him…
Enduring the pain, the bloodiness of my purple scalped thighs.
I couldn't imagine
How my skin—was buried
With the boy's body under the grass.

  *   *   *

Each interval of his slow steps to the altar
Followed by the organ's sounds of Bach,
A mystic flash of lightning shivers through his body,
While snuffing out the smoky candles,
As the boy's skin was shriveled by blazing fire—cremated,
And over the altar are burning time's ashes.

2006

THE MANSIONS AT NEWPORT

> *Lucky Newport! Three poems for you, never-silent town,*
> *were dedicated by Longfellow.*

Merry Christmas! — Newport of Rhode Island,
Queen of America by "The Gilded Age" of your land,
Step by step along the spectacular Newport Bay,
The very best living accommodations, "summer cottages"
That money could buy...
You are born for a Christmas Festival — Newport,
Inviting the ice sculptors from the Maine snow
And people dining in elegance aboard a luxury rail car,
Celebrating evening Christmas at the Mansions — everyone
Visiting the summering place for America's wealthiest
Of the "Golden Age"... A dramatic powerful impression!
History you can touch: Italian marble castles,
          richly colored and decorated
Louis XIV and Renaissance style, early American colonial architecture,
The gilded bronze chairs and chandeliers,
          the mahogany cabinets, the carpets,
The image of butlers, parlor maids, footmen, gardeners...
But... owners? What about rococo-dressed rich men and women?
Oh, they were not all happy!
While visiting the marble mansions
You, as a tourist, can listen through earphones
To the secrets of the family generations:
"The lady of the house, who did dress her monkey
In a Tuxedo... Insisted and forced her daughter
To marry a Duke against her will..."
        So, my dears,
Their money couldn't buy everything!

2006

The Last Soldier

Monuments tremble
When a veteran dies…

I didn't know, indeed,
That two or three miles from my home
I breathed the same air with
111-year-old Anthony Pierro of Swampscott
Who died February 2007 — his final battle.
The last living Massachusetts veteran of the World War I.

111 years — three digits — God's spirit is three in one.
Born and raised in Forenza, Italy,
He moved to the United States in 1914
And later — to inscribe himself into the history —
Served in France with the 82nd Division
AEF, 320 Field Artillery.

111 years — three digits as three stars
Hung on the chest of Anthony's war jacket
A uniform with jodhpurs, combat boots, canvas leggings,
Half-bowl helmet with a visor…
On his shoulders — a bedroll and a wooden rifle with a bayonet.
Soldier-of-the-army-corps-khaki-green-gray!
In Arlington Cemetery — the grave,
The marble Tomb of the Unknown Soldier — is trembling,
                                    Remembering…

111 years — three digits — three legends.
Over three generations
This is the strength of the nation,
This is America's soil.

2007

The Place where I Live

"Ocean Shores Apartments" —
An old brick castle with the parapets of a fort
Resembling centuries past — a guest
Setting to rest
At the beginning of the causeway to Nahant,
A reminder of the old-fashioned cow-pasture beach,
A reminder of the old Lynn-Nahant friendship…

Surrounded forever by the white ocean foam and the green grass,
Framed by the clear blue of the Atlantic sky
Saying every day: "Good morning!" to the sun
When it bounds up from the deep ocean.
At nighttime the red bricks murmur — a silent lullaby to Egg Rock
Shaking in slumber between the waves.

An extension of the people themselves,
Surviving the severe winter, the snow, the cold, the whirlwind,
But on a spring day — the ocean, a breeze, a breath
Even a sparrow song can heal…
Every season brings a new scene:
In Feb. 2004, on the iced coast, a little seal
Directed its melancholy black bulging eyes
To the eight-story building's windows.
If only she knew the many grandparents watching with compassion.
In mid-January 2007, a western yellow bird — Wilson's Warbler —
Flying coast to coast — winging at the garden's trees
Of the "Ocean Shores…" — like a good omen!

This tower, where old people grow older and slip away;
Petite great-grandmothers and grandfathers
Live with memories — remembering jobs, wars, hurricanes,
The old dear houses, verandas — the milkman…
Proud men and women who raised children, danced and sang,
People who are thankful, rejoice and pray and cry "Alleluia!"
Nature is at work… in those apartments:
Healing, comforts, wheelchairs, walkers, oxygen, fire-alarms,
                                                encouragement,
Parties, *God Bless America,* singing group and dancing,
                                       bingo, voting, enthusiasm,
Walking, swimming, fishing, tennis, yoga, cat and doggie ladies,
Gardening and flower, *Red Hat* women. Flea markets,

Do Leave Out My Right Hand

Movies, computer games, cards, entertainment, photographers, trips,
The community room breakfast and coffee
A pot of ethnicities, cultures and races:
Irish, Jewish, Russian, Italian, Greek, Chinese,
                                        Polish, Armenian, Albanian,
A place to share love, care, compassion, anecdotes, choices and company,
Old fashioned clocks ticking,
                         grandmothers' pictures, antiques and jewels…
…At night—the moon sliding by the windows
Tasting cooking from the ladies' kitchens,
The usual visitors:
Doctors, nurses, homemakers, children, friends,
                                    nursing home and death.
Veneration for all old women and men who died,
Remembering the death of Gloria McDonald, the advisor of
The Ocean Shores Club—who became an angel so fast!

Our house!
A spirit castle that breathes
Through the inhabitants' hearts, minds and art.
At number 808, Ms. Sima Chernyak, all day long from her window
Paints the picturesque views of blue-red-orange-pink-white:
The changing colors—light and shadow—
                                the landscapes of clouds and sky
From sunrise to sunset in the forefront
                            of the outlines of Boston skyscrapers.
At number 210, Ms. Sheila Scholl composes music,
And sings songs at her piano… Drawing—her second hobby…
Many others sing… At number 706,
                   a gentleman plays Beethoven on the piano…
…Seated at a small table, near my open balcony—at number 718,
I write verse after verse…adoring the view
That opens before me…
…The white sailing yachts—sliding into a summer silent sea…
…The bronzed moon—pouring gold in the fall evening ocean…
…The indistinct sleepy blur of Nahant in winter…
…The spring pink horizon line that divides
   The blue-red sea from the blue-black sky
      Penetrated by the seagulls' scream
         That takes away my dream
            In a green-blue morning air…
               Here I became a poet!...

2007

Keeping The Light At Egg Rock Island

> *Tenderly in the stern of his skiff, George Taylor, the keeper of Egg Rock Lighthouse laid the shrouded body of his wife... He was taking it ashore for burial... She had died on the lonely island, of the coast of Lynn, during the winter. Unable to provide burial in the rocky soil, he had placed the body in the oil house carefully wrapped in blankets.*
> Daily Evening Item, *Lynn, Mass.*

4 March, 1860 — I was cleaning my veranda
When George, my childhood friend, stopped by...
— Hi...Effie...,— he said saddened — I just buried my wife!...
Breathless, I shook his hand... embracing in sympathy...
Tightening his fisherman's cap in his hands, he sighed:
— My gal... it is loneliness there, on the Rock... pain... dark,
If you could desire to marry me...hurry...decide!
I must return to the Light before dusk!
No woman in the universe could consent in just seconds...!
But me...
Thanks to Thee,
A tragedy brought a husband to my altar,
The sanctuary of my heart
Belongs now and forever — to Egg Rock Island
Where my man, George, is the keeper of the Light.
The minister who had buried his dear lady,
One hour later — at a Lynn church — crowned our marriage.
I became George's second wife.
No veil, no flowers, no guests — only my trunk.
He must return to the Light before dusk
He must return to the Light before dusk.
We two entered the skiff
And rowed through the Nahant waters
Sitting on my bride's wooden chest
Enclosing my belongings, my dreams and my holiday dress.
I lifted up my head — A small black cloud
As a bad sign — slipped away.
While the white clouds
Like wedding flowers
Ran with us... Ran with us...

Our family at the Lighthouse — all seven, a biblical number:
George, me — Effie, the dog Milo, the ocean, the sun, the moon and God!

Do Leave Out My Right Hand

Blessed by the symphony of the fluctuating blue waves
And the myriad sounds of birdsongs and buzzing bees,
The only entertainment — watching the white seagulls
Dropping their clams on the rocks
One — two — three times...
Midnights... middays... a Queen, I guess... I was
Of the monumental Egg Rock — which more than an egg,
An elephant could be...
Our Light guided and warned mariners,
Greeting cheerily and waving hands
When their ships floated near us...
Proudly, a ship called the Mayflower came to our island
I sang *Amazing Grace* at my piano as a welcome!

Nine months later — in a severe November rainstorm
My first baby girl was born.
Before her arrival, George sculled to Nahant
To find a nurse — but they couldn't get back!
Alarmed, panicked, alone on my stone island
I kept the Light trimmed and burning bright.
Meanwhile I delivered my baby in the oil house
Where long ago my husband's dead first wife had lain,
Where she blessed my four other children, boys and girls,
                                                                      coming in a row
All with blue eyes — painted by the waves and the skies.
Here ends my story — now a legend...

      *   *   *

147 years later, evening, June 2007,
Sitting with my Nahanter friend, Ms. Effie Taylor, 86,
Near her house, on the Nahant shore — glancing at Egg Rock.
Complete darkness... Lighthouse no more... obsolete,
Today everywhere — automatic lights.
Egg Rock — as an abandoned, dormant mammoth
Watches in envy the romantic yachts — alongside...

Effie... the fifth generation of the Taylor family,
Concentrating on the silent, gray stones —
Prays for her great-grandmother
Whose honored name she holds...
In Effie's bright blue eyes
The Light of Egg Rock still shines...

    2007

Lucky Day — 07-07-07

Saturday, morning, 7:00, July 7, 2007 — Lynn, Mass
On the TV — Channel 07 — the weather points 70°F,
A baby was born 07.07.07 —
                  weight 7 lb. 7 oz. — time 7:17 — 7th floor of a hospital
While numerologists give their illustrations:
7th year of a new century
7 days — a week in the calendar
7 notes — music in a scale
7 colors — in a rainbow
7 wonders of the world!
007 — the famous serial movies
Lucky 7 in the gambling machine…
Today many Massachusetts residents travel to Foxwoods, CT
Or float on a Casino Cruise… Good Luck!
Also Good Luck to thousands of new couples around the planet
Who celebrate their weddings on 07.07.07.
Happiness and hope — on their nice faces on TV
What beautiful smiles…

07.07.2007 — Lisbon Official Declaration Ceremony of the
7 New Wonders of the World
Announced by actors H.Swank, B.Basu and B.Kingsley,
7 Wonders, 2007: The Great Wall of China, Petra, Chichen Itza,
The Statue of the Christ Redeemer, the Colosseum,
                              Machu Picchu and the Taj Mahal,
More than 100 million people worldwide voted.

All in all — Al Gore, the former VP —
From seven years' work and an Oscar later
Comes alive in his *Live Earth* Global Concerts on all seven continents
To play over a 24-hour period on July 7, 2007
London — Johannesburg — Rio de Janeiro — Shangai — Tokyo —
                                    Sydney — Hamburg,
Including "Nunatak" music group from Antarctica,
Bringing together 100 musical artists and two billion people —
A movement — to solve the climate crisis;
"An Inconvenient Truth" culminated by "7"…
                    seven, sete, sem, set, siete, ziben, shtate…
Today — 07.07.07 — the whole green world smiles with you…

2007

ST. MARY — AUGUST 15, 2007

This Day in History:
In 1057, Macbeth, king of Scots
Was killed in a battle by Malcolm.
In 1769, The Imperial Bonaparte was born.
In 1945, Japan's Emperor Hirohito accepted
                            the ending of the World War II…

Today, Wednesday — 08.15.07
Up there — in Space
An astronaut ends a space walk
After finding a rip in a glove —
        Repairs are made.

Down on the Earth — in Iraq
The surgeons repair the people wounded
        From deadly bombings.

Under a mountain in Utah, Crandall Canyon Mine
After a collapse — six trapped miners — six spirits
Lost in dark, in silence, in cold soil…
Mine rescuers running out of options.

The meteors of the August night's sky — remind us
The anniversary of three icons' deaths
Mother Teresa, Princess Diana, and Elvis Presley…

While on TV — Martha Stewart's Parade
Of the 2007 Happy Wedding Couples!
Meanwhile, parents and children
Joyfully buy
Going back-to-school clothes at the Mall…
The world repeats and repairs itself, and goes forward.

2007

There Is a Flag in the Air

Old Glory!
Today — September 6, 2007 — 3:00 P.M.
America has one more Flag!
Rising from our 8-story building, Ocean Shores, Lynn, Mass
Awe-inspiring for Ocean Shores' veterans
From World War II, Korea and Vietnam…
When Bruce Dobson — a Vietnam veteran — raised the Flag,
It was lifted up together with the veterans' hearts!
Followed by Richard Perry playing *To the Colors,*
Trooper Foley and residents singing *The National Anthem*
"God Bless America Again!"
On the top of the flag pole — the Red, White and Blue
Enhanced by the ocean, white with foam,
The first fluttering — from the Atlantic wind — south to north
Echoing the sentiments of monuments throughout the country
Waving and murmuring America's victories!

Solemn moments, attitudes, memories, honors, songs.
The veterans saluting the colors.
Left hands rested on the canes — right hands at the foreheads.
The Mass officials stand to the right, hands over their hearts,
The aged tender tenants stand at the salute
Singing *Amazing Grace* with tears in their eyes.

  *   *   *

My scarf — flag-like that envelops my chest
Brings me back to my old country:
My mother had said that
When my father — a USA immigrant
Came to Albania to marry her in 1930,
Among many gifts he brought was an American flag.
Years later, to hide this flag
My mother quilted it between two blankets
That covered my childhood bed when I slept.

I shake my scarf…I raise my head…
There's a Flag up in the Air
There's a Spirit up in the Air…

2007

"FOR THE BEAUTY OF THE EARTH"

To Rev. Teri Motley

I am Teri Motley — with the Spring, I find myself
Today — 04.19.08 — at Nahant Village Church, in Mass.
Where I desire to become a minister of The United Church of Christ.
I believe God, as the Holy Spirit,
Was and is with me. He appears in the beauty
Of natural harmony,
And cares about humans and humanity.

As a girl singer, when I sang the *Sanctus* from Bach,
I did not know who was calling me.
As the boy Samuel said: "Here I am!"
Here I am! Lord! —
My spirit pulsates today, in the culminating hour
When the Ecclesiastical Council votes —
And the Nahant Church bells toll for me!...
Answering questions from the Council's members,
The answers, received for 2000 years from others,
I am full of tears — remembering
My own life's most difficult problems and emotions,
But God's love helped to sustain me through the pain.

— I am a creature, not a creator,
And my life is intended to be centered on God!
Jesus died a human death to save us.
The cross to me is a symbol of
"Truth forever on the scaffold — Wrong forever on the throne."
I believe the Resurrection is God's victory over death,
That Jesus has a relationship with me personally,
Jesus has walked with me in times of my suffering,
And Jesus calls me to be ordained to the ministry.
In the Church to which I am called
I will invite people — proclaim the Good News.
May I be given the strength, the wisdom and the faith
To serve God this way.
AMEN!

April, 2008

Amore Mio[*]

Let my life grow
        Through you.
I will wait…
If you can't come to me
I will come to you,
Even if the Sun never rises,
Even tho' waters dry up in the sea,
Even if the cosmos collapses,
Even if white oleanders do not bloom in the spring,
Even when solemn death closes
My eyes.
Triumphantly
I will come to you,
I will come to you,
Amore Mio!

   2008

---

[*] My darling

The White Mulberry Tree

Running in the century's horizon,
We are both weathering
An unexpected June hailstorm
Shielded by a white mulberry tree
Whose leaves feed silkworms.

No matter.
The sky strikes us with stone pieces,
Tearing our garments and gowns.
My darling—we weave our silk cloth of love
Embroidering with our hearts' magic yarns
Decorated by a garland of hailstones
Melting in the perfumed air
From the berrylike fruits.
Then, when the storm is over,
Our woven cloth of love—will cover
Our bodies,
And we shall run again,
And we shall run again
Straight
Through a thousand summers.

June, 2008

THE TENNIS-PLAYER GIRL

Who is she?
Her player friends call her Judy.
Wearing flowery, short pants and sneakers,
Jumping and running around the tennis court,
She plays, she laughs, and she shrills,
She uses the racket and tennis ball
As a juggler would.
The sound of the girl's rising tone —
With seagull screams over the ocean
Usually steals the afternoon naps
Of a 95-year-old woman nearby:

"Who is she!? Confound her!"
Thus, at half-past three
The aged woman appears at her balcony,
She sits so slowly, she rests, she waits, she dreams,
She says things to herself.
A memory comes to her mind
Of when she played tennis in the past,
Uniformed with white
In a pleated short skirt — like a butterfly!
Oh!... Her life - a blink of an eye!
The teary-eyed lady — feels tennis-arms.

Judy's voice cries out to the high heavens,
The elder lady changes her curse and sighs:
"So much joy! Shout out – my dear Judy!
You – vivacious girl! – Your lilting voice
Brings spring to my painful days..."

Could one aged woman play tennis?
No, but she keeps watching from her high balcony.
All she loses are her afternoon naps.

2008

08.08.08 – Man And Nature: Harmony

Three eights in a row
Spells good fortune in Chinese culture:
Friday, August 8, 2008 at 8:08 P.M. – XXIX Olympics preview.
China began the Beijing Olympic Games
An impressive start at Bird's Nest Stadium
Like a giant Bright Light.

Symbol-spirit-dream-magic
2,008 drummers lit by strobe lights,
2,008 dancers in glowing green suits,
2,008 men in white robes doing Tai Chi.

History and a new century!
China in a New Light
The center of a Universe
Letting the world inside
The Bird's Nest Stadium.
Beijing put on a history lesson.
Four billion television viewers
Watched in Awe!
The Game's opening ceremonies
On a fantastic height filled
With dragon pillars and Tai Chi monsters
The greatest show on Earth.

How far we've gone with technology!
Long-sought Olympics spectacular

Extravaganza of fireworks,
A huge translucent globe in the air
Dramatizing its ascendance
FINE CHINA!

As the crowd gave a thunderous Welcome
The Chinese said Welcome – in English.
President Bush

Offered the athletes inspiration.
The first U.S. President to attend
Olympics on foreign soil.

* * *

Yellow state,
Red Capitalism,
A Mao Tsei Tung portrait.
Sleeping giant
Equilibrium forward...
17,000 Beijing couples were married
On this Good-Luck Day!

* * *

08.08.08 — Chinese Civilization!

An Alchemy of peace
GO CHINA! Symbol of harmony!
Sing: "One World, One Dream!"
A message of Good Omens!

2008

The Telephone

Your telephone is dying
While you speak with me!
Or is it at its end like
Your soul's battery?

2008

"AVE MARIA" INTO THE MRI

Agony to enter
The MRI environment,
Removing all metallic objects from my body,
But not my prayers from my shield of the faith.
Like a somnambulist, I am led by a technician
Who helps me lie inside the MRI screening tube.
I will never forget his encouraging look.

    The magnet is on; my claustrophobia too.
Noises — deafening.
Lights — blinding.
Sounds — I vocalize with a fading voice:
Ave Maria — Gracia Plena
Benedicta tu in mulieribus…
Ave Maria — into the MRI tube
Ave Maria — my crying voice on the Earth below and the sky above…

The golden clouds descend over me.
I Feel her wondrous love.

    2008

To My Husband

    1 + 1 = 1
You plus me = A one month fetus.
You plus me = A 9 month fetus.
You plus me = A human being,
    1 + 1 equals 3
Who broke the arithmetic rules?

2008

THE RED HAT LADIES

> *"When I am an old woman I shall wear purple*
> *With a red hat which doesn't go, and doesn't suit me.*
> *And I shall spend my pension on brandy and summer gloves*
> *And satin sandals, and say we've no money for butter."*
> Warning *by Jenny Joseph*

So, the 21st century began
With a framed "Warning" poem and a red hat
That American ladies sent to each other
As a "birthday gift" – decorating ideas
Which triumphantly and enthusiastically
Led to the birth of the "Red Hat Society,"
Spreading later to all corners of the globe.

Wearing the purple outfit and red hat—
They are hot.
Greeting middle-age and up to 100
No rules—no ills—no pills
Only Fun!
I met the vibrant Margaret Brown—a kind lady—
"The Queen Mother" of her
Red Hat Social Club somewhere in New England.
Dressed in red jackets and red hats,
The same color as her female compatriots.
They put a red hat on my head
And holding each other's hands we sang *America The Beautiful*.
Their idea of love, life and changing time—A philosophy
for trips, restaurants, plays—
                  dancing, singing, playacting, laughing, ballgames:
"I don't care if I never get back!"
There are illnesses and deaths
In the Universe,
But there are no thoughts of these things
Under a Red Hat.

Every Valentine's Day, Mrs. Brown's ladies visit an indoor garden
"The Butterfly Place"—Westford, MA.
Hundreds of free-flying butterflies

Descend over the ribbons, flowers and roses of their Red Hats
Inspiring them
    How to fly
        One after another
           As angels
                Into Paradise.

2008

THE GOLDEN EPOCH

A new immigrant from Albania
I shook hands with black people
(they were kind)
For the first time in my life in America.
I voted for a black governor
For the first time in my life
In Massachusetts – The Commonwealth
In the 21st century (November 2006)
Yesterday, I voted for Obama, our 44th American President.
(Mrs. Freeman, black woman, 92, prayed:
"Dad, Mom, I'm going to vote
To make a black man our president!")
America can't stop smiling!
Surreal day. Mythic day.
Washington D.C. January 20, 2009
The trajectory of history removed
The slave's shackles from Obama's right hand
When he took the Oath!
"Thou Who hast by Thy might,
Led us into the light…"
(The Negro National Anthem
Quoted by Rev. Lowery, in the benediction
At President Obama's inauguration.)
At noon in America
One journey ended; another began.
American eyes shine
With Obama's Victory
In Lady Liberty's torch!
All Hail to the Chief!

2009

The Last Prayer

> *Omnis Spiritus*
> *Lavdet–Dominum*

In silence.
In the blank church.
(No believers. No candle-flames. No priest.)
Madame Regina prays.
She prays the black pearl rosary
Ten *Hail Mary*'s… one *Glory be to the Father!*

She wanders day by day
In and out of her Catholic church
Closed for financial reasons.
She used to be a helper — and she still thinks she is,
She kneels before the altar
Where Jesus Christ suffers on the cross,
She prays her old rosary
Stringing her life events together
Looking back — remembering — praying:
"My Lord — 96 years ago
I was baptized in this church
Here —
My matrimony…
My children's, grandchildren's and great-grandchildren's baptisms,
My confessions…
Eye to eye with you, God,
And my blessing for eternal life
Here, I want to die!"

    * * *

> *Ora pronobis peccatoribus*
> *In ora mortis nostrae.*

On a sunny May sanctifying Sunday
The last breath — And
The last prayer of Madame Regina
In the empty sanctuary:
"My life lies exhausted in my church.

God be at mine end — Extreme Unction!
...I pray for me... I pray for me...
Ave Maria!..."

2009

Memorial Day Mitsubishi Sale

It begins with shadows
The 12.07.1941 Japanese air-raid on Pearl Harbor
Torpedo planes attack — *Nevada (BB-36), Arizona (BB-39),*
    Tennessee (BB-43), West Virginia (BB-48), Maryland (BB-46),
    Oklahoma (BB-37)…
Japanese Mitsubishi planes — bombing
Covering the port, the ocean and the sky
In flames, grey and white curling smoke — alarms, explosions, noises,
Killing and wounding soldiers — heart-shaking…
Something left forever — In the sea
And in the air!
Today smoke rises in Nevada, Arizona,
Tennessee, West Virginia, Maryland… in every corner of America
"Invaded" by Toyota and Mitsubishi cars of the Samurai
Publicizing safety-security-comfort…
    In a
"Memorial Day Mitsubishi Sale!"

   2009

FRIENDSHIP

> *Kogda soldaty p'yut vino…, poyut*

President Obama and his family
Visited Russia on July 6, 2009.
Coincidentally — the same day
The choir named *Fargenign*,* of Russian-American immigrants
Performed a concert north of Boston
Singing Russian songs of the Second World War
And American lines of William Kils:
"When soldiers drink wine…, they sing"
(*kogda soldaty p'yut vino…, poyut*)
. . . .

The 21th century stretches its cold legs
To warm — in the 20th century's fireplace of charcoal,
But finds only ashes remain.
So let us drink and sing in harmony for friendship.

2009

---

* Happiness

09.09.09 — Lucky Number

Today — nine leaves on the maple tree
Became red.
The Maine lobster's price went down.
09.09.09, Wednesday — my appointment with Dr. de Venecia —
At Mass. Eye and Ear Infirmary — his prescription for 99 pills.
At 9:00 AM — Martha Stewart show: "*Pack your Own Lunch* Week."
North Korea marks anniversary — youths dancing.
Nine — the number of completion.
NASA's Hubble Space Telescope
Rebuilt by the astronauts — in the universe somewhere.
Sudanese woman journalist — freed after
Her conviction for wearing trousers.
In our church, Rev. Titus advised — don't shake hands
To prevent catching H1N1 (swine flu).
Today, in Boston — generations of fans
Take gaming guitars in hand — to play like the Beatles.
Today: 09.09.09 — numbers align for weddings:
Nine couples in Hollywood spend 99 cents
To get married at a 99 Cents Only Store!
Today: A copy of a Robert Frost poem:
"The Road Less Traveled" and white roses
Were placed on the late Edward M. Kennedy's Senate desk.
The day 09.09.09 ends
With President Obama's speech — urging Congress
To overhaul the expanded health care coverage.
Time is flying supersonic…

2009

THEY ALSO FACED THE SEA

There is a small historical city in the United States:
Provincetown, MA — on the hook of Cape Cod.
The first broad breath of Massachusetts
Where the Pilgrims' Mayflower touched land — November 21, 1620.
Visited through the centuries by
Vikings, Pilgrims, Pirates, Painters and Poets…
Who built the nation's oldest art colony.

You, a visitor who passes there, after adoring
Whale watching, merriment, alluring horizons, beaches and dunes,
Turn your head to the Harbor — that of Fisherman's Wharf
Where five large black-and-white photographs —
                                                each a dramatic portrait
Are mounted on the walls of an old grey building.
Five Provincetown women of Portuguese descent —
Waiting and watching… far away… the sea…
Their teary eyes, white hair, and deep wrinkles —
Each a portrait of Cape Cod fishermen's mothers and wives
Who kept the community alive:
In death, in birth, in grief, in mirth — the Pilgrims' continuation,
In the everyday struggle to feed the family's togetherness,
Knitting, hooking and braiding rugs, needle working, spinning,
Working as nurses, teachers, and telephone operators —
Let us bow down with respect and gratitude
To all of those who were, and still are, America's mothers:
The iron backbone of a country's civilization —
Pouring into the soul of this great nation
Resistance, attitude, art, majesty, and continuity…
Yesterday, they faced the sea — today the world,
Their lives — a map of humanity.

2009

Drinking "Cobra" Beer

An October night.
The chill air spreading across my balcony
While drinking a King "Cobra" beer.
The premium malt liquor—a golden spirit
Spreading through my body,
Becoming a spell in my blood.
Drinking – yet looking at the sliver of the moon,
A moon playing the flute
Bewitching me.
The flute resounds
The Cobra's profile—snake charmers
Into the basket of my veins.

Please, flute, do not pause
Because
The Cobra jumps on me.

   2009

Sacrifices — Candles Doused

The first News Item:
"Today, 31 May 2009 — a praying day!
Dead, a 97-year-old woman — the last human alive
From the Titanic catastrophe in the Atlantic in 1912."
(Her ashes poured into the ocean — reuniting…)

The second News Item:
"The same day, 31 May 2009 — a disaster!
An airplane, Air France 447
In the Rio de Janeiro — Paris transit
With 228 people on board
Sunk to the bottom of the Atlantic ocean."

Perhaps —
This tragedy is mythical —
A dark vigil of Neptune?
For the Titanic's aged lady
Atlantic sacrifices
The black waltz of the ocean…
It's difficult to put into words.

2009

LOST

The last chapter of my book
Dedicated to my dead, beloved husband,
I finished on 06.05.08 — I walked along the seaside
Tear-worn, tired, thrilled — to find "our" bench.
A blind old lady, well-dressed, was seated there.
I poured out to her all my heart's despair…
Resting on her white, blind stick, she consoled me:
I am Jeanne — When I married, my husband asked:
"Jeanne, how long will you love me?"
"For ever and 'a day'…, my dear!"
He died recently.
And I said to my son on "Father's Day":

You are "A day!…"
In my next book…

2009

CON MAN

Enjoying coffee on my veranda—adoring the ocean,
Morning—March, 27 2009, at 9:00 A.M.
My cell ringing—unrecognized voice:
"Madam! Congratulations!
You won an $8,000 Fox Fur Coat!—If... If... If..."
I hang up the receiver—leaning over the railing, asking:
O white Atlantic waves—did you hear that!?
Oh, Yes! We listen every century – the same tales!
For example – 8000 years ago,
Just on the shore where your modern house stands,
One tribal man lured another with a fish
When his friend approached
The bad tribal man hit him with stones
To grab his... outer covering, the white gold bear skin.
When did the concept of confidence begin?..

   2009

Remembering Longfellow

1. Longfellow Bridge

All alone—Monday, November second, 2009,
Walking on the long Charles River bridge
That joins Boston and Cambridge,
Surrounded by skyscrapers and yellowish leafy trees.
Above, in the blue sky float a few white clouds
As pink cruises slide off onto the teal-blue Charles River,
The shining water full-of-fall-red-dead-leaves, like tears,
A balmy breeze smooths the green poster, "Longfellow Bridge"
Named for him—The Nation's Honored!

In his days the poet visited regularly this bridge
Attracting the attention of the passers-by,
Walking and reciting his verses with rhythmic steps:
"Gazing with half-open eyelids,
Full of shadowy dreams and visions,
On the dizzy, swimming landscape,
On the gleaming of the water,
On the splendor of the sunset."

I rest on the rusty, thick, old, iron hand rail
Feeling the bridge noise shaking from his steps—absorbed
With the clank of railroad trains,
                        cars, trolleys, trucks, bicycles, pedestrians,
While "Boston Duck Tours" swim under me.
O Birch tree! Growing by the mystic Charles River!
In your white-skin wrapper—writing a good hand
"The Song of Hiawatha"—unforgotten narrative.
Save it forever…

The poet's ghostly figure follows me near the banister.
It murmurs, repeats, and whispers still,
Fragments of verses chased by steps and by wind,
That shall echo forevermore!
O young girl! In sports uniform and ear phones
Stepping along with the music's melody on the Longfellow Bridge
Send the poet a wave.

2. The Nahant Summers of Longfellow

"The tide rises, the tide falls,
The twilight darkens, the curlew calls
Along the sea – sands damp and brown
The traveler hastens toward the town,
And the tide rises, the tide falls."

Perhaps, this "evening of life" thought
Was written of Nahant beaches by Longfellow
In their summer sojourning with his second wife, two boys
And Harvard friends. Boarding in the cottage of the Johnson family.
The sunny summer days Henry swam and walked on the shore,
Watched the surf and the white sails between the blue waters
Breathing in the wild pink roses' aroma.
Evenings on the veranda, with books and friends, chatting
Reciting poems of *The Seaside and Fireside*
He wrote inspired by the brilliant Nahant sunset.

During his summers in Nahant, Longfellow came down to people,
Meeting fashion-gloved arms-elegant ladies with big fancy hats
And tail-coated gentlemen, adoring him: "Our Nahant Poet!"
Reading his tale *The Golden Legend,* or visiting Swallow's Cave.
If he wrote for the heroic,
He could have tea with the former President J. Adams,
If he felt despairing and lonely,
He might find himself sitting in the moonlight – looking to the sea
Nahant was his "Treasure Island" – shimmering through his poetry…

The poet left Nahant the last Sunday of August 1851.
The last August Sunday, 2004,
I am sitting on Nahant's south shore, between the ocean and the forest
At the foundation stones from Johnson's house
Under the shadow of willows, the poet's pleasant trees,
Reading *Evangeline* – over the ruins and the grass
Listening to *Druids of eld* – those prophetic Gaelic priests approach me:
Sighing, "Henry Wadsworth wrote his first large expression, here…"
This is the forest primeval. The murmuring pines and the hemlocks.
Bearded with moss and in garments green, indistinct in the twilight,
Stand like Druids of eld… … …

. . . .

Loud from its rocky caverns, the deep-voiced neighbouring ocean
Speaks, and in accents disconsolate answers the wail of the forest.

The Nahanters joined the Longfellows
In Sunday singing at the Nahant Village Church.
I go every Sunday to the same church, rebuilt,
He is seated near me — I see his profile — praying the lines
Of *Christus,* statement of his deep belief, his highest inspiration.

The tide rises, the tide falls,
Printing the poet's name on the sands…

3. Thank You — Our Poet!

I walk along Nahant's oak-tree-lined streets
Reciting from *Tales of a Wayside Inn,*
Astonished by the magic of his art
"I for ever!" — *The Saga of King Olaf*
Yes, you *are* for ever — O King of verses — Henry Wadsworth.
O magnificent ballad-singer! — O national bard!
Not just America fits in your heart,
But the whole planet.
The worldwide epic heroes' poet
Familiar with Europe — Longfellow.
Even my country — Albania,
Praising our nation's hero — George,
Who vanquished the Turks with his dazzling sword.
Your verses — a hymn's impetus — incited the Albanian people
Fighting the Ottoman Empire for freedom.
Your "Scanderbeg" inside *Tales of a Wayside Inn* is immortal!

I, an Albanian daughter
Recite those verses with the rhythm of my spirit
Repeat with the centuries: Scanderbeg… Scanderbeg,
Remembering Longfellow — Our Poet!

2009

"It Won't Be the Same"

> *We, non-communist people, who lived behind the "Iron Curtain"*
> *in East Europe hoped and believed in the Kennedy brothers.*
> *We felt that they were our saviors, directly or indirectly.*

The race...
December 8, 2009 — Tuesday morning.
I am going to vote...
To fill the legendary seat
Of the late Senator Edward M. Kennedy — the Lion of the Senate!
Held by him for half a century —
We will miss his roar!

On the first page of the Boston Herald — his possible successors:
Four Democrat candidates — portraits dreamily smiling:
Michael Capuano — Stephen Pagliuca — Martha Coakley — Alan Khazei,
Four foes scramble...
To continue the "Massachusetts Spirit" and solve its needs.
In my ears sound the phone calls
With the warm words and promises of the candidates.

I am going to vote.
There is a chill wind in the air —
A bright-blinding cold sun
My eyes and my face are wet
From the plink-plink drops of the fir trees' melting snow
Imprinting on me — this historical event,
The second Ted Kennedy funeral,
The family still grieving.
("The King is dead — Long live the King!")

I am going to vote... substitute
E. Kennedy, who 13 months ago voted for Obama.
Ms. Regina, a Hyannis poll worker remembers.
The old lady, a long time friend of Ted, bellowed, moaned:
"Going to the polls this time will be very sad...
It won't be the same!"

I am stepping into the Church Street polls — "Amazing Grace"
"To vote" again for Ted Kennedy...

2009

"Merry Christmas Nahant"

The last verse of a Longfellow poem dedicated to Nahant

Seven nights before Christmas
In the evening – December 19, 2009 — the roads
Of Nahant — flashing with lights —
The annual Christmas Parade — deafening
Full of cheers, car horn noises, carol melodies.
Nahanters salute from the walkways
In front of their decorated wreathed doors…

On such a night — a Christmas Party
At the almost 200-year-old Jenkins' Hill House
Invited the islanders celebrating…
Seated near the fiercely burning fireplace,
I am attracted by a huge lady's portrait
In a large gold ornamental frame.
Her dress striped green and gray
With a delicate white-lace open collar,
Wearing a diamond brooch.
She looks at me with dark brown eyes,
Her face rose-red from the fire's waves:
"Welcome to the Jenkins' house" — her voice echoes —
"If I could, I would be playing this mahogany piano
As I once did on a Christmas Eve.
By chance, as a ghost, as a little bird
I fly tonight in awe! — to the Christmas tree
Where the unseen ghosts of this aged house
Become the white angels
Enjoying the party from their green perches…
A cup of the red Christmas wassail punch — the old style,
I have the desire to drink, to wish:
Blessed are you Nahanters tonight in this place,
The past is never dead!"

I elbow through the crowd — the party guests
In the three big living rooms,
No music, no dance. Only conversations.
Cavaliers' red pants and bow ties; elegant ladies in backless gowns —

Standing, stepping, meeting and toasting each other
With crystal wine glasses — meanwhile chatting and laughing...

There are antique objects in this museum house,
Like old and new telephones — cellphones that men
Put in their pockets — the wiggling-blue lights shine
Like a handful of fireflies...
The past never dies:
A perpetual Christmas memory on the rock island
In the 21st century dawn
And centuries from now.
Merry Christmas Nahant!

2009

The Northern Lights of 2010

Winter wake up with an Olympics symphony!
02/12/2010 — The XXI Winter Olympics in Vancouver, B.C.,
Canada — The world's second largest country — invited
2500 dazzling athletes from 82 countries, all-star-games
    (Even skiers from Ghana!)
The Olympic rings — illuminating the ocean
The B.C. Stadium roaring with evening extravaganza
Cross-beams of torches — an obelisk of "Welcome Planet" —
Burning and radiating over the earth — the Olympics Light!

Snow — the natural medium
Technology — man's push for ever more speed
Success or death?
Nodar died making his first attempt — in the Olympic spirit!
The opening ceremony dedicated
                      to the memory of this Georgian athlete.
A cluster of yellow daffodils.
A 21st century madness.

At the fir mountains,
Photographers, international TV crews, a spectacle
View pictures day-by-day and sport-by-sport
Alpine skiing, ice hockey, biathlon, downhill ski jumping,
                            ski-cross, curling-hurricane,
Floating rotation, jumping style in the air — a gallant race,
Challenging human and geographic gravity
Majesty!
Giving the world a natural smile.

Even the eye of the wind watches
The joyful — the cheerful — applauding youngsters shaking bells
The iconic Canadian maple leaf
Painted on their faces.
Compared scores! Championship!
Ski- jumping athletes — As Mother Earth pushes them up!
("…I fly with skis in the sky! — I am blessed here!
I can hear people crying!
The Globe — so small! I can jump, circle it around.")

Vancouver, beat the drums of victory
Echoing the centuries.

Wow! — women's ski cross!
Higher! — let's do it!
Upside down — amazing flight!
Anxiety! Tears! — (save drama for your mama!)

Side by side the skiers,
The last kilometer — the final line,
Victory!... champagne!
A gold medal inspires! — share the podium — Native Hymn!
A violet-ribbon bouquet with green flowers
From a green planet!

The world today is Snow White
Boys and girls — figure skating — ice dancing,
Artistic and high-strung
Kneeling down and kissing the ice after challenging
The passion, love, stunning style and spirit
Romeo and Juliet have descended from heaven gardens to Canadian ice
Dancing, loop jumping, music,
                      blessing in words of different languages.
Thank you, Canada!
The world's people this day are in the "Canada Start House"
Go World, Go...

2010

Stopping by the Train Station on Valentine's Day

The Boston sky sends whiteness and wind and dancing snow.
I take the electric stairs — slowly
Down the Park Street Station — descending
Where the fast trains fly
With red hearts — away
On this Valentine's Day!

The stairs, the walls, the people's faces and hands
Have gone red.
Even the half gloves of the poor old man — playing
On a Havana guitar — are red…
He sings — sighing the red love words,
The same sound of the subway's
Erotic dream, murmuring still.
The romantic angels — dancing
Over the young couples — boys and girls — embracing
Arms tightening around each other like statues!
Every kiss — love's elixir.

I am sitting in the Red Line train
In front of a young Chinese boy and his girlfriend,
Holding and squeezing each other's hands.
The boy — like a plant sprouting from the soil
The brown-eyed girl — black, long, heavy hair
Covering her face — exposing only her fresh, red, heart-shaped lips
That unfurl myriad roses' scented petals…
On her white jacket's sleeve — embroidered with pink numbers — 3333.

Question: — Where are we going on these subways?
Tuck-tuck…the train of time disappears in the tunnels
Maybe to the center of the earth?
Maybe 3333 years before, in the past, or 3333 in the future?
      However…on both sides
Love rules and leads till the end of time itself.
Love, Ljubov, Amore, Dashuri, Sevda, Sesy, Sagapo, Amor, Yeu…

L o v e — nothing else — L o v e!

2010

Visiting Amish Cemetery

Plain and simple graves.
No flowers, no bushes, no trees.
So small and so tight beside each-other...
With handwritten names — carved on cold stones:
Mosses C. Kopslund Jr.
Born Jul. 6 — 1892
Died Aug. 9 — 1970
Age 78 Yrs. — 1 Mo. & 3 Dys.
    Rachel L. Wife of Mosses C. Kopslund
    Born Mar. 9 — 1896
    Died Nov. 5 — 1981
    Age 85 Yrs. — 7 Mos. & 27 Dys.

Oh, ye, blessed Rachel and Mosses' ghosts
O, ye, walking, laughing, singing across
The sweet aroma of broad cornfields — watching granddaughters
Over the windmills
Cleaning, feeding and milking cows.
O, ye, grabbing a dark dress and trousers
Hung out on the clothesline — drying in the air
O, ye, driving the horse-drawn buggies clip-clopping everywhere.
Oh, your spirits guiding at night — telling chilling Dutch tales,
Following fireflies — with twinkling lights
Until they get tired — lying in the grass
Covered and wrapped by a white-cloud-quilt-sky
White — as Rachel's girlish tiny cap
Dreaming the existing world of Amish life.

2010

ACTING NEIGHBORLY

Coming from Albania,
Ben's grandmother
Visiting him and his sweet wife,
Seated near the window, asks:
    "Who is your neighbor?"
    "We don't know them!"
Early in the morning
Grandmother bakes a bread with raisins
Divides in two — a native ritual —
Puts one on a plate
And going straight to the next-door neighbor
Full of generous goodwill.
Instantly, a big dog comes from behind — attacking.
The injured old lady lies on the cement —
Her bread behind: "No trespassing" lays.

Calling the police — the owner
Describes the scene he saw from the window:
"…An old, shrunken homeless woman — stupid,
Dressed in black — came right onto my property…"

    *   *   *

In the Emergency
Sad Ben and his wife — holding grandmother's hands.
"Did she make a mistake?"
In agony, she moves her lips — sighing:
    "My beloveds,
You must love your neighbor as yourself!…"

    2010

I Had a Wife

to Mr. Gerald

She was beautiful,
Her voice—a nightingale,
She was a holy creature.
She died at 87—two years ago.
We were age mates, match mates, soul mates…
I sold the house,
And now I live in Apartment 608.
She was beautiful—Yes!
Now I shake these skeleton keys,
The only memory remaining
From my old childhood house.
Those keys nobody needs—useless,
Like the owner that holds them in his hands…
I had a wife,
She was beautiful.

2010

Unspeakable

He called long distance, saying:
"Do you know about the kabbalah?"
He couldn't say: I love you!
"Yes, I know" — I said.
I couldn't say: I love you, too!

He sighed: "Do you know about
The oldest letter written from any human being?"
He couldn't say: I love you!
"Yes, I know" — I murmured.
I couldn't say: I love you, too!

He asked: "Do you know that in Maine
Portland Harbor has 365 islands?"
He couldn't say: I love you!
"Yes, I know" — I whispered.
I didn't say that I dream of living,
One day, on each of Portland's islands
Each day to write a letter on that grass and bird island
Under the lighthouses: fogginess, sunshine, moonblue, rainstorms,
Closing the 365 letters, with:
    I love you, too!

2010

MOTHER TERESA DESCENDS AS A SAINT IN 2010

> *"By blood, I am Albanian. By citizenship, an Indian. By faith,
> I am a Catholic nun. As to my calling, I belong to the world.
> As to my heart, I belong entirely to the Heart of Jesus."*
> Mother Teresa

2010 — 100th anniversary of your birth.
100 candles lit all over the globe.
Your immortal face would have appeared in news,
Announcing your centennial celebration,
As You spent your life
Cuddling the dying and the abandoned,
Carrying the weight of the cross onto your small shoulders
In Calcutta's streets and wherever humans breathe,
Treading the globe — as a Good Samaritan —
On your misshapen small feet in old patched brown sandals
That today rest in the museum at the Vatican.

Mother Teresa — the proof
That the soul purifies itself as much as
Its closeness to the holiness of God.
O Mother — O lantern of love!
You encoded the connection of your spirit to God
In your body and in others
By picturing heaven into people's souls
In innumerable avenues of Love.
Now you reside in paradise — sending blessings —
    Haleluia!

2010 — "The Mother Teresa Year" — You are present:
Books, pictures, movies, monuments, memorials, museums,
Concerts, science symposiums on every continent;
USA Postage — your portrait on stamps.
In Albania, your face on gold coins,
In Kosova, *The Cathedral* was built in Your memory.
Once, as a little girl, you wrote poems in Albanian,
Sang hymns in the church choir
              with your mother, Drande, and your sister, Agge;

Then The Lord chose thee to build a house for the dying —
You left your parents' house,
Dedicated yourself to *Missionaries of Charity, Nirmal Hriday, Sisters of Love*
To cleanse the face of Earth
Of disease, wounds and poverty…
A small nation's daughter —
With a small flower's name, Gonxhe (Flower-bud),
(Now, a new white tulip from Holland is named after You.)
A young bud fused into the sufferer's veins.
Named *The Mother of a big world, The queen of humanism, Nobel Prize!*
Your white-and-blue-striped cambric robe —
A symbol of your spiritual value —
No comparison with ladies' strewn garbs.

Mother Teresa,
Mother Albania — yours and my common homeland —
Gives me the right to decipher the hieroglyphs
Of furrows on your face — cut by tears
Of thousands of Albanian mothers:
One of them, my own late mother — now 100, like You.
(In our capital, Tirana, I kissed your cheek and your right hand
While you blessed me with your left hand on my forehead).
Teresian virtue — the sinless humanity —
Nurtured — by our birthplace's tradition of self-denial
At the beginning on Illyria's ancient lands,
An ancient part of Albanian genes
Echoing and revealing civilization's first morning…

Mother Teresa,
Came into this world, helped;
Sometimes, she struggled in vain.
Now she works
From heaven.
Caritas et amor,
        ibi est.

2010

TRANSLATIONS

from Nase Jani

I'll Tear Apart All that I Haven't Written

i hate
my love lyrics

i'll kill them and tear them apart
i'll throw them to the silence of the tomb
i'll damn and forget 'em
they drive me crazy

they drive me crazy without me getting crazy
they make me decay without me getting dead

i'll throw them to the soul's tomb
i'll strangle and tear them
this is what i'll do

i'll chase the soul from the soul
the brain won't produce a verse anymore

i'll take myself by the hand
i'll make me walk on the sidewalk
not to get knocked down by cars
i'll make me sit down on a wooden bench
i'll give me a rosary to say
that i may live without living, without love poems
that's what i'll do.

i'll close my eyes
not with my hands,
but with stones, with slabs of tombs.

i will not see
why should i see, who needs sight anymore?
the world — a thing, i — something else.
i'll shun him, who i was
not even myself will see,
a crazy not-crazy
a decayed not-dead
living without living,
without love poems
i lost myself without finding me.

i'll strangle and tear apart
all that i've written and not written

only my soul escapes
isn't it dead yet?
doesn't my soul lie in its tomb?
doesn't it lie with me any more?

i'll tear apart
all that i haven't yet written.

2009

TO HER

Did I see a spark in your eyes?
Let them be bright...
Did I see a smile on your lips?
Let them smile...
Did you hide your grief?
Let it be hidden...
Did you pour out your spirit?
Let it pour...
Did you undress your body?
Let it be undressed...
Did you turn off the light?
Let it be dark...
Did you forget yourself,
Let yourself go...
To the top of the mountain
Let yourself go...
To the bottom of the sea
Go deep...
In the waves of your heart,
Let yourself drown...

And wake up
After midnight...
To breathe to me a little voice
If you could...

2009

I Trudged on the Bridge One Night

I trudged along the bridge
In the night…
The river was dry like me,
In the night…
I waited — sitting on a stone,
In the night…
The night was no more — It was I…
The night…

2009

HE IS I

tie him up,
he is crazy.
tie him up.

he is I.

kill him,
he wants to be human.
kill him.

he is I.

don't give him a tomb,
he'll germinate love
don't give him a tomb.

he is I

2009

THE ALBANIAN LEGEND OF ROZAFAT

"DO LEAVE OUT MY RIGHT HAND — I AM STILL ALIVE"

To my infant grandson Jan, half Albanian, (nursed on the breast milk of his Albanian mother) with my desire, hope, and wish that he will grow up to learn about and love Albania.

Stone — Albanians' hereditary mastery;
Stone — nobility;
Stone — metaphor and legend;
Stone — song and lament;
Stone — men's oath;
Stone — fine art!

1

For three days and three nights
Thick fog fell mysteriously over the Buna river
Covering the lake and Shkodra city.
A fogginess never seen — even by the old folks.
The mist, as white tongues of a thousand dragons,
Outstretched and knitted with the trees' branches,
The houses, people's hair and their limbs
Making them walk blindly and fearfully,
Becoming irritated, moving arms and hands
Into the emptiness of a terrible, impenetrable fog bank.
While scared dogs barked with squealing sounds
Foreshadowing the misfortunes —
A catastrophe about to happen —
The ruin of the high castle
At the top of the steep hill — right there in the south side of the city.
Even though three brothers
Promised to build a strong citadel
And continued for thirty-eight moons, twelve days...
Daily the stonework was built up
Nightly it tumbled down,
An unknown force dismantling
The big corner stones — pushing the walls like an avalanche
Down the hill into the chasm,
Dancing rocks with horrifying, fearful violence
Raising in the air a white cloud of lime and dust
Covering the leaves of the trees.
And the men, alike —
Dusting their auburn hair — becoming three phantasms
Working unceasingly around and up,
While a wild, cold and gray wind dries
The blood of their grasping hands
And sounds the alarm... Why?... why?... why?...

2

On the fourth day the fog disappears and is buried
Between the sky's hollows and river's mouth.
Three brothers climb hopelessly and nervously
To the top of the hill — to begin
The ill-omened castle one more time.
They are three qualified masons,
Famous for their masonry, stone-cutting and decorating
Brilliant houses, towers, temples and palaces
Giving harmony of form to all the area's buildings.
Aren't their magic and skillful hands
Injured, skinned with scrapes and nicks,
Using the silver hammers like jugglers
Until the pounding monotone noise reaches the sky.

. . . .

Just as they touched the stones and the mortar,
A gray-bearded man appeared — as if sprouted from the earth
Dressed in a long pleated cloak —
So long, it covered his sandals.
A tuft of white hair shook under his worn fez
He looked so tired — resting in a tree branch,
Casting his white eyes at the three brothers,
Greeting them with a solemn voice:
"Hi, there! How is work going?"
"How can it go when the walls
Built in the daylight
Tumble down in the nighttime?" — asked the older brother
"If you want to raise the walls,
I'll tell you the secret means." — he sighed.
Three masters' hands approached the stranger.
The first brother thought, "He might be a fortune-teller
Seeing a message in a mutton joint
Or hearing it in the murmur of the willow's leaves."
The second brother was terrified
Looking at the old man's walking-stick
Twisted in a coil as a black snake.
"This mystic old beggar might be a magician…or worse…"
The third brother — bowing with honor,
With a lilt in his voice — inviting:
"Welcome from your antique land, our guest,

You must bring a word from a goddess."
The old man crossed his hands on his chest
Rolling the white eyes to the sun,
As if asking its permission:
"Alas!" — he spoke with a mournful tone —
"My message is not a blessing!..
I'll be as a sinner…"
"We swear on that sun," — said the older brother —
"Let the deadly sin alight on our spirits."
"It must need a sacrifice."
The old man whispered with a quavering voice,
"My lads, not one noble thing comes easy
On the earth — without a sacrificial idol.
To build a strong castle
That will stand up to the enemies' attacks
Century after century,
You must place a young woman from your family
Into the foundation…"

A dead calm, a dead thought, an uncontrollable
Moment — did alarm the three confused brothers.
How could this sainted man propose such a barbarism?
"I am reading your hearts,"
Said the white-haired man, rolling his white eyes
To the sky — "But, know, the divinity itself
Has consecrated the walling-in
As a rite to the good of humanity.
Now, whoever will be sacrificed is destined.
I know you are three married men,
And your three wives are at home.
Every day one of them brings your lunch;
One of the three who will be fated by the goddess
Will deliver the food at tomorrow's zenith of the sun
And will be walled within the stones."
He scooped with his crooked stick in the soil — seizing a stone:
"Put your three right hands over this rock —
Men's oath on a stone is stronger than others.
I beg you to be faithful in not telling your wives;
She must be innocent of all intentions."
"On this stone let us swear, swear, swear!"
The three brothers' voices — vibrating in the humid air,
And the wind blowing harder and louder,
Howling SACRI… FICE… fice… ice…

3

In dark, in terrible shadows, three brothers
Riding horses back home — with the image of *her* death
Bringing them to grief
A deathly thing — the cause of their despairing.
"A corpse without a grave" — the horses' trot refrain
"A corpse without a grave" — the horses' trot chime.
"Tomorrow we shall know" —

. . . .

Their mother and the three wives waited in the cold air
Worried about the day's stone work.
The brothers' hearts answered nervously — "Say nothing."
By custom, the mother ordered the three daughters-in-law about,
Helping husbands clean their exhausted bodies
And drying their long auburn hair
With homemade red-striped towels,
Every red line — the resemblance of the striped skin,
The bloodied and hurt sweet wife.

"Dinner's ready" — proclaimed the old gray-haired woman.
Three wives brought
A low round wooden table with small stools to the fireplace.
When all gathered around the board,
They put on the husbands' bosoms the red cotton napkins
Reflecting again their bloodied figures in the men's eyes.
The chimney corner smells of burnt tree stump
And just-baked steaming wheat bun's fragrance;
The salted curd, bean porridge, smoke-dried fish — on the table
Then the old mother put a ram's shoulder on the oldest son's plate.
Mystical? Frightening? As if he read the ram's bones,
Finding there gore or everlasting love…
"I can't eat," — murmured the first brother in a shaky voice
Hiding from family members, he gave a signal to his wife
To go up to their solitary bedroom.
The second brother — nearly cried with his stricken heart, added:
"I'm not hungry either… going to sleep" —
                              mouthed the words to his wife.
The third brother didn't touch any food at all,
Watching speechlessly his wife, Rozafat, washing the dishes
And later, in the barn, helping her milk the goats.
The old mother never ordered the two other daughters-in-law

To milk the endearing bright-black furry goats;
Acting restless, the daughters cursed them and slapped their backs —
Only sweet-voiced Rozafat — talking, singing and
Using the fresh beech leaves to entice her she-goats.
Tonight, while she pressed and soothed the animal's udder,
And the white milk squirted in the sheet-iron pail,
Her husband eyed her two breasts, bloated by human milk,
The only holy, vital meal of their cherished little child.
He extended his hands to reach and embrace her face despairingly.
She found herself surrounded and enclosed by the animals
Using their strong horns to protect Rozafat from anyone touching her.
"Alas! — A foreboding!" — the husband cried in horror,
"Destiny has chosen her... she'll never see another night."
The third brother — as pure as the driven snow,
Downcast and bitterly sad, sat under a starry sky
Listening to confused sounds of the wind's voices: "Boy,
The solemn promise and disloyalty are sleeping both
Tonight in your rocky turret." The blowing wind
Yelled: "Confound them!"
Observing carefully his brothers' bedroom windows,
Two small hollows in the thick stones
Like two wild beast's eyes that
Gleam in the darkness... silence of the grave... "How they..."
A shade of doubt crossed his mind.
Then Rozafat approached with reverential awe:
"My lord... are you in trouble? Why is your face
Turning yellow just like tonight's moon?"
"For how long," — he sighs, "have we been married?"
"Three green springs... did you forget my lord?"
Staring innocently into his eyes — a tremor in her voice —
"Why? Maybe some eerie events are coming..."
"No!" — he stopped to catch his breath,
"My beloved, my godsend Roz... it's time to go to bed..."
His face turned bloodless, murmuring, "I will not breathe a word."
But he couldn't set his mind to rest.
A timeless bird flying under cover of night crying.
Rozafat looked at him fixedly... "Yes, a foreboding!"
The wind struck her golden curls whispering, lamenting:
Roz...roz...oz... You are Lost...lost...ost,
And slammed on the windows' shutters foretelling
The echoes of the women crying and weeping.

4

The new day began.
In the firmament rose the sun.
The builders' mother cooked their lunch for them.
Wheat bread, ram's meat, fresh onions and sheep cheese
Putting all on a large copper tray.
After stirring the red wine in a gourd bottle
She ordered the first daughter-in-law:
"It's your day, my dear, the husbands' food to bear."
"I can't," she said, "Ah, mother, all night long
I felt ill…pain, weakness and great sorrow."
The fox's tongue spoke in her mouth.
"Get well soon, my oldest daughter."
Then the mother-in-law commanded the second:
"My sweet daughter, the men are hungry and thirsty, go quickly."
"My honored mother," — she pleaded, —
                            "I'm going today to visit my parents
They have waited for me for weeks, please!"
"Have a good trip" — wished her mother-in-law — and shouted:
"My little girl, Rozafat, do take the road
It's getting hot, my lads can't wait, it's late."
"My son is asleep," answered the third, guileless Rozafat
Shaking the child's wood cradle.
"Don't worry, young wife, I'll care for my grandson."

. . . .

Rozafat left with a big baking pan upon her head.
Step by step accompanied by the wind
That toyed with her blue ribbons and sang:
"What are you holding over your golden curls? Why?
Ah, Roz… it is your death's dinner, meat and wine,
Unluckily, you'll never see your home, your child,
                            and the finished castle
You'll never see the sun, the moon, or feel your husband's embrace."
Under the force of the full May sun, walking in a daze
Rozafat listened to the forest birds choir
Twittering, longing and lauding her flower-beauty,
She stepped happily on yellow daffodils' petals

Surrounded and followed by bronze butterflies
That begged her to cut her errand.
She strode by the mountain spray
Where the crystal water frothed from the red stones
With happy sounds that vividly reminded her of
Her first unforgettable chance meeting
With her future husband…
Sitting on a purple rock by the spring
She set her imagination in flight…
…back to a May day sunrise,
When she was filling her wooden jug at the rock's water
Up galloped the thundering horse hooves —
Between the trees' chiaroscuro a young horseman appeared.
He approached, but the girl didn't turn her curly head
"My horse Dory and I are thirsty…don't be afraid,"
He said, without getting out of the saddle
In the water's mirror observing her prettiness.
Her beauty is as the dew of the pink sky.
"I welcome you stranger" — her voice as the spring's gurgling
She held out two soft white hands, giving him the wet wooden cup,
Two sapphire blue eyes — reflecting her high spirits
Becoming easy prey of his dark green eyes:
"The prince I always had dreamed of,"
Her little heart danced,
"I'll leave no stone unturned — to marry you,"
Repeated his glance.
She felt for the first time love's shudder, love's secret.

. . . .

The sound of churning water now takes human form —
…She froze…
Her husband's desperate face waving under the cold pond's water.
"A foreshadowed calamity," she whispered,
Wailing and getting up from her sweet dream.
She took the road straight to the miserable hill and Hell
Pushed by the frightful sounds of the wind echoing like a death knell.
Walking in the forest and gazing at the sudden black clouds
Rozaf shuddered as she passed by creaking trees,
Her eyes filled with unshed tears.

Sunless, in shadowy glimpses, sad,
                         the meditative young wife took courage:
"Enough! Let's go to the dark world… if necessary…"
Climbing on the hill's Nob, seeing the four horizon points,
Turning her face to the valley, the green gardens of her house,
She prayed: "Good bye, ah, my ancient motherland,
My home, my family's hot hearthstone.
                         Good bye, ah, you, my neighbors,
My relatives, my friends. Farewell, oh hills and plains
Olive groves, flowers, trees, and you, oh desolate alley
Which my feet tread for the last time…"

5

When Rozafat appeared before the men
In a long white dress and sleeveless, heavy black woolen cloak
With blue ribbons in her golden curly long hair
Flying in the air by a spring breeze,
Her husband fell down half-dead.
A breathless pause until
The two brothers-in-law said sadly:
"Oh, our honored sister-in-law,
You are fated to be walled up now!"
And the sky did fall upon the ground.
The trap is resolutely set!
The forlorn bride quivers with fright,
Mouth and lips dry with despair,
Her spirit a violent ocean wave.
"It's time, it's time…" —sighed trapped Rozafat—
…"It's time to ask for a favor."
Held by the two brothers' hands,
The bitter tears streaming down her face
She cried, "Please!… wait, please!…"
But they don't wait… they grab her
And lay her down on black slabs of stone
And work fast,
Faster than time,
While she lets out a mournful cry
That pierces the sky.
As, with arms flailing, she tries to defend herself
Against the stony-hearted men…
She craned her neck and reached for her husband,
Shadowed within this nightmare.
Meanwhile, his heart melted with pity,
Her face became whiter and whiter
Breathing heavily, screaming, imploring:
"Please, don't cover my right eye—
I want to see my son.
Don't cover my right hand,
I need it to caress him.
Do pull out gently my right breast—

Do Leave Out My Right Hand

I must feed my little child.
Do leave out my right foot,
So my baby's cradle I can rock."
Her voice grew weak from begging,
But reverberated from the stones, rocks, the olives' trunk, the earth,
From the sky, from the half-pale moon and fiery sun
Adding to and echoing her last agonized wish:
"May my bosom be strong
May the castle be solid
May my son be intrepid!"

. . . .

They fixed mortar and stones
Around her supple figure
Half enfolding — as she had ordered.
When her brother-in-law with his trembling hands
Hesitated to put a small stone
Over her half-exposed head,
She moved her free right hand upward
Placing the stone herself, covering the left side of her face
Relieving the men's anxiety… adding to the building
More and more stone work…
The work was done. It was a dying day.
The wind was driven like a ghost
Rushing down the olive hill and rills
Followed from time to time by the angry sun's needles of light
Shaking and frightening the earth.

6

Half immersed, half dead, Rozafat hallucinated,
"...Am I still in breath or in death?
What happened to me?
Some strong hands have built my grave here.
I am asking you Lord, are you watching me?"
"Yes," — answered the black-gray stone above her,
"All the world, and all the skies, and all the centuries
They know of your sacrifice in the wall, but
Forgive me my weight just over
Your little heart, forgive us
You, white rose — pretty Rozafat."
"I forgive you." — she said drowsily,
Running her right hand over its sharp edges.
The tearful chorus of stones offered her friendship:
"We carry the earth's fossils' story.
In our core pulse the sounds of
The first morning of creation.
Stay with us, endure, like us, the cold
The heat, the rain, the loneliness,
And you will live forever."
Lulled by the stones' gentleness, Rozafat plunged into visions:
...An army with tired soldiers appeared
Covered in dust and mud from head to foot.
Their helmets, spears, shields and swords
Were heavy on their injured bodies.
"What is this solemn march of war?" she asked,
"Must history repeat itself?
Whose image is its leader, an old combatant, highwayman,
Coming from ancient times to appear to me?
The squalling wind is blowing his long hair — Hi,
I am Rozafat!" —
"Yes, I know my child!
Your sacrifice will be read in the nation's eyes,
In history's passing we Albanians
Have been, once in awhile half dead,
Occasionally half alive — like you, Rozafat.
Nevertheless, even the half-dead we struggle,

And will struggle for centuries,
We are either coming from a war
Or going to another war..."
The fighter drew a sword and placed it near her hand,
Saying in an ancestral voice, "You are my soldier."
"Am I?" — she whispered —
"When needed... We Albanian women are strong spirits,
When needed... we offer sacrifice again...
I am still alive..."
A few light melodies and girls' voices passed by,
"Who are you, touching my cheek?" she asked,
"We are the mountain nymphs
To freshen your face with the flowers' dew,
To comb your hair and to prepare you
To act as your mother, sisters, friends
Offering our lament, our pain, our praise."

7

Her face is luminescent white.
The nymphs embellish her hair with lilacs,
Staying near, silent and solemn
In this sorrowful, painful darkness
Begging, "May this holy tomb
Be known as a reminder everywhere
Of this woman's milk which is dripping.
Let it keep flowing, never stopping
How could she forget her nursing child?
Let milk keep flowing
Over the stones of the fortress.
Let every tear
Be a memory of Rozaf-martyr,
Echoing constantly the mother's cries and laments
The foreseeing of the prophecy:
Many tears will be shed on Albanian soil
Until the sacred river Buna
Becomes flooded by the teardrops of the Albanian mothers…
Let the hill echo her love…
Let her dreams be alive and fly…"

. . . .

The castle's stones continue yet
Remain heavy over the martyrdom of the young woman

> Immortal eye
> > Immortal hand
> > > Immortal breast

The castle still stands huge on the hill
Watching wistfully over the lake and Shkoder city,
Its walls looking straight ahead to the sky.
Like the sun, Rozafat rises and sets.
While the stones weep and sigh
And never stop shedding tears.
The bare bosom, stony, white
Hangs forever like a stalactite,
As slowly it emits droplets of milk.

And ribbons of blue blossoms grow along its base,
 Forget-me-nots…
Continue blooming down the centuries
From every angle of stone,
Bowed and bent forever
By the light breeze from the lake—lamenting and
Echoing—learning by heart
The name of ROZA… ROZAFAT…

Katerina and Nikola Cheku, paternal great-grandparents of Rozi, in the village Dardha, Albania

Lefteria and Theodhos Cheku, paternal grandparents of Rozi, in the village Dardha, Albania

Katerina Lacho, maternal grandmother of Rozi, in the village Dardha, Albania

Peter Lacho, maternal grandfather of Rozi, in Millinocket, Maine.

Aleksandra and Pandi Cheku, the parents of Rozi

Rozi in village Dardha, Albania

Rozi in High School in Tirana, the capital of Albania

Pandi Cheku, the father of Rozi, violinist in an orchestra in Detroit, Michigan.

Rozi's father on the VULCANIA's trip to Albania and back

Rozi and her husband Viktor Theohari, with their children Diana and Akil, in Tirana, Albania

With Albanian writers (from the left) Helena Kadare, Ismail Kadare, Fatos Arapi, and Rozi, in Tirana, Albania

Rozi — graduation from North Shore Community College, Lynn, MA.

With College teachers (from the left) Kathleen Gerecke, Rozi, Diane Kendig, Joe Boyd, and Marilyn Dorfman

Daughter Diana with her husband Michael.

Rozi with her grandson Jan Sommer

Rozi singing in the Nahant Village Church chorus. The first row, second from the left

Rozi singing in the *Fargenign,* the Russian chorus in Lynn, MA - first row, first from the right

Rozi giving her book to Congressman Eliot Engel in a meeting with Albanian Americans in New York

Albanian Consul S.Kochi and Rozi meeting Edward Kennedy. Rozi is presenting her poem dedicated to the Senator.

Reciting poems

Singing Albanian songs with two older brothers, Theodhosi and Kicho (with guitar), Swampscott, MA

At the *Red Hat Society*

Writing verses for the American flag

Albanian flag raised at Boston City Hall on 11.28.2009.
Rozi reads her greeting to Albanian-Americans.

AFTERWORDS

SENSE AND SENSIBILITY IN THE LEGEND OF ROZAFAT

Gjekë Marinaj, College Instructor
Translated by Peter R. Prifti, San Diego, California

It is not easy to determine all the factors that influenced Rozi Theohari to choose Rozafa as the leading heroine of her most recent book. The title of the book, which is totally in harmony with the subject of the work, is Rozafat. When one takes into account her self-confidence regarding her chances for success, plus her experience and professional strength, one is led to believe that she was aware of the difficulties she would encounter, in her attempt to throw a new light, both in a conceptual and ethical sense, on the personality of Rozafa, and the society in which she lived. In order to better understand the philosophical message of the author, let us consider the following two verses, which are tinged with a poetic tone of protest.

> *"A corpse without a grave" – the horses' trot refrain*
> *"A corpse without a grave" – the horses' trot chime*

The chief "credit" or "blame" for these "golden orioles" of the author, in respect of herself and Rozafa simultaneously, is a matter of secondary reflexes—namely, the instinctive inspiration that sets the creator in motion, as a result of the internal push that comes from contact with something unusual. After reading about the extraordinary sacrifice of Rozafa, Rozi, too, decides to indulge in an act of sacrifice, and that is the perceptions of others toward her initiative to renew one of the best known and most popular legends in our cultural arsenal. That which, at first glance, might seem like an unconditional embrace by the author of the incomparable heroism of Rozafa, undergoes a transformation without any visible strain, which enables the author, now in complete control of her ideas, to modify the legend.

The book awakens interest especially with regard to the symbolic concept, as well as the reflexes of the syntheses of sensibility and sensitivity that characterize the leading heroine, after which the legend is named. Naturally, in the process of recreation, one can detect significant borrowings from the inherited versions of the old popular legend. This has been attained by adapting the essence of the legend with professional responsibility. By so doing, Theohari distances herself, on the one hand, from those who perceive her as an imitator, and on the other hand, from the traditional perceptions that others have about the legend of Rozafa. There is wisdom in such an action, since otherwise the reader would be left with a sense that something is lacking, no matter how accomplished the legend is from the standpoint of mythology.

Perhaps this is the reason why Theohari, has emphasized the psychological and social aspects of the legend. One can also see here some new layers, namely elements of the analytic progress of the legend. We are talking here about the feminine frame of reference, whose injection into the tale is, on the whole, the product of Theohari's spontaneity. The feminine fragility and sensitivity in Theohari's poetic arsenal, as manifested in this book, is conjoined not only by depth of thought, but also by an imaginative spirit. This can be seen in the following two verses:

> *The sound of churning water now takes human form*
> *...She froze...*

In her efforts to regenerate the feminine potential of Rozafa, the author transplants to her something of her own authorial personality. The desire to remain faithful to the warm intonations inherited from popular legends, has enabled Theohari to maintain a correct stance, with regard to the expression of her authorial energy. It is precisely here that we see how her emotions wrap around the legend with the same regularity that latitudinal and longitudinal lines wrap around the terrestrial globe—thin defining lines, which nevertheless are imaginary. Let us consider for a moment the first two of the following three verses. Those represent the popular tradition, whereas the third line is attached lovingly to them as a decorative label that comes strictly from the author.

Farewell, oh hills and plains
Olive groves, flowers, trees and you, oh desolate alley
Which my feet tread for the last time

Theohari demonstrates in her work that she is fully knowledgeable about the literary mechanism that drives the imagery of Rozafa's tragedy. She puts that knowledge at our service as readers, and at her own service as author. Her work in the book Rozafat persuades one that by grafting her ideas on some of the bare branches of the legend, she rejuvenates the basic notions of Rozafa:

The trap is resolutely set!
The forlorn bride quivers with fright,
Mouth and lips dry with despair,
Her spirit a violent ocean wave

Naturally, it would have been too heavy a load on her shoulders, to succeed in such an endeavor. Therefore she turns for help to the Albanian psychology of the time, insofar as dealing with the spiritual issues and the consciousness Rozafa needed in order to carry out the act of immuring herself. In such a social universe, the worldview of Rozafa is presented as an act that was in accord with the ethical codes, and the one-sided civic interpretation of the time which, in one way or another, was shared by all of mankind.

No. Rozi Theohari is not so open as to directly ask such questions as: Why was it essential that a woman be walled up, when each one of the three brothers fulfilled the criteria suggested by the old man, as the indispensable condition for the construction of durable walls for the castle? Neither does she openly challenge the laws for giving a woman (or denying her) the right to oppose her own immurement. In contrast, the means chosen by Theohari to explain the absolute control of males over females in the Albanian culture, pertains more to the "metabole" model in mythology, than to the natural history of the epic in our legends.

The poetic transformation that we find in the treatment of the most challenging social problems, in connection with the figure of Rozafa – viewed as the core of the legend – sheds a new light on symbolism, imagery, characters, or even style. Furthermore, they are necessarily linked to only one culture or generation of men. The contemporary reader should understand that the legend is rewritten in support of, and not in opposition to present-day society.

Most certainly, this does not mean that the excursion by the author into the original forms of interpretation, has no bearing on the recollection of the chronological, logical, or even geographical order of the events that take place in the traditional version of the Legend of Rozafa. We know that many writers have done research with professional dedication on the conjunction of relations between legends and mythology, on the one hand, and on the other hand, the society which has preserved them to this day. Theohari does not attempt to depart from this sort of research method. She does not even try to deny that Rozafa is an inseparable part of a given period of time, and a given society, and that by the very nature of her self-sacrifice, she remains a typical legendary product of the Albanian specimen:

Like the sun, Rozafat rises and sets.
While the stones weep and sigh
And never stop shedding tears
The bare bosom, stony, white
Hangs forever like a stalactite
As slowly it emits droplets of milk

Features of this sort make the creative world of Theohari unique. Her readiness to reveal her convictions and social outlook regarding ethical and historical issues of this kind, is indicative of the sincere relations she wishes to have with Albanian readers. Although the heroism of Rozafa has been dealt with by other authors, in particular by Kadare, Theohari is the first female, as far as I know, who has dared to displace Rozafa from the podium of antiquity, and set her on the stage of contemporary judgment –where she herself becomes a judge of her own heroic act – and makes a correct diagnosis about certain males who, to this day, suffer from the sickness of chauvinism, in their relations with females. If, in the work *Rozafat*, Rozafa displays contradictory sides of herself, in order to keep peace with the men in her household, Rozi decided to take on the role of her interpreter, and why not even that of her lawyer in the court of society, against all those who still wave the banner of superiority vis-à-vis the Albanian female, and even the women of the world?

The focus on the human element in the process of artistic creation is a plus in this book. In its pages are unfurled, in an ambivalent manner, the relations of humans with the natural world, and the consequences of those relations for our culture.

As one who knows well the ancient culture of her country, Theohari combines the imaginative and scholarly factors without confusing the concepts that run parallel in them. The legend of Rozafa gives us to understand that the world of Albanian legends has given us not only a powerful and enchanting legacy, but also enables us to grasp the means by which ancient Albanians tried to understand themselves and the world in which they lived.

To elaborate on what I said above, by clothing Rozafa in a new suit of human instincts, the author broadens her vision by bringing out into the open the colors, tastes, feelings and sentiments of the modern Albanian female. We are accustomed to a "manly" Rozafa, who sacrifices herself without expressing any anxiety that her life is ending. This is the Rozafa whose only vocal anxiety is her child (when she pleads that the baby be allowed to suck her breast), and that the walls of the castle stand firm. True enough, Rozi Theohari does not openly reply (if someone were to ask), whether Rozafa accepts her immurement because she considers the castle's walls more important than her life, or the life of her child without a mother, or her husband's life without a wife, or yet again because she was aware that any protest of hers would have been useless, since her husband and her brothers-in-law had already finalized their plan to vanquish her. When I say that she does not reply openly, the reader should perhaps infer that she leaves the question open-ended, so that he may understand that writers and poets, too, have certain prerogatives, when it comes to the christening of their ideas, based on facts. Nevertheless, she tries to center herself as much as possible, as she moves between fact and fancy.

Theohari fashions her answer within the bounds of reason, as she sees it. Naturally, one must grant that she runs into another difficulty here. It's common knowledge that Albanian legend and mythology are complex, by their very nature. Yet, they have survived, by virtue of their inherent beauty. From this perspective, the book logically is literary rather than academic in character. Hence, it should be pointed out that in this book Theohari, in fact, serves merely as a transmitter of this legendary energy. Fortunately, she performs this task in a totally novel and enlightening way.

Lastly, let us consider the verses below, which are purposely cited here in order to support the thesis of this introduction. Here, the author bares her emotions in a direct and translucent manner, both in the evolution of her thoughts, and in the way she expresses them.

Rozafa yells:

> *"Wait, Please!"*
> *But they don't wait…they grab her*
> *And lay her down on black slabs of stone*
> *And work fast,*
> *Faster than time,*
> *While she lets out a mournful cry*
> *That pierces the sky*
> *As, with arms flailing, she tries to defend herself*
> *Against the stony-hearted men…*

These verses should suffice to conclude this literary essay. At any rate, I would like to repeat once more that with her most recent book, Rozi Theohari, brings to us a strange epoch that is totally alien to us. But, on the other hand, she has rewritten a well-known legend, concerning which there are questions that have not been fully answered either in her book, or in the books of other authors. Of such questions, I would single out these: What makes people go to such extremes as to wall up a member of the family? Why do we allow ourselves the freedom and capability to defend such a custom with so much vigor and passion? Where exactly should the line be drawn between the humane obligation to oppose, and the desire to allow sacrifices like that of Rozafa? Furthermore, was Rozafa's demise an act of immurement or self-immurement? The reason that Rozi Theohari gives us only her own thoughts, and not any factual data, with regard to these questions, is not difficult to surmise: She is Rozi, not Rozafa.

Our Best Citizens
by Kerry Zagarella

In honor of Rozi

Explosions and liquor
toast our independence
while we sit in plastic chairs made in China
and casually discuss politics
and throw away leftovers
We are an affluent nation
the poorest among us no match for the hungry world wide
we have become lazy about our freedoms
fat ignorant consumers have become the new age drugged out hippy
A people too preoccupied
            by getting the next new bargain or gadget to be a citizen
The government loves you and your bumper sticker patriotism
                                that passes for pride
God Bless America
These colors don't run
This country love it or leave it
While cigarettes and trash fly out of the cars
Decorating the highways and streets
What will it take to make us citizens
We have teachers, they are the new immigrants of our land
Searching for a better tomorrow and finding it
they feel the pride of citizenship as a gift
Rozi as a young girl in communist Albania
slept under a quilt that her mother made to hide an American flag in
Now when Rozi speaks about our country, I listen
She is a patriot, invited by Lady Liberty
Rozi didn't know those many years ago
her family dreaming of coming to this country
that she would arrive as a teacher
reminding us what it is to be an American

Thank you Rozi…thank you

"Ms. Theohari's writings have always offered much joy and educational information, as well as unconditional love and friendship that come from her spirit, as an author and person. She has been named "The spirit of Albania Diaspora's creative journalism."

Bota e Gruas Shqiptare, *Albanian Women World* Group.

Rozi Theohari came from Albania to America in 1994. In her country, she received University degrees from two different institutions, one in Literature and the other in Economics. In 2000, after mastering the English Language, she received an Associate's degree in Liberal Arts at North Shore Community College in Lynn, Massachusetts. She is a member of Phi Theta Kappa, an International Honor Society. As a high-achieving student, she was nominated to the Dean's List in 1997-1998. She has published her poems in local newspapers and in poetry anthologies. She also publishes constantly in "ILLYRIA", the Albanian-American newspaper in New York. Her accomplishment as a writer in English comes from her experiences in her native country, where she published several books:
    2002, a collection of poems in English, "Two Halves";
    2003, the old Albanian legend "Rozafat", English and Albanian;
    2004, a novel, "Lajthitje Dimerore";
    2005, a collection of short stories "Mbi Thinja Fryn Ere";
    2006, a collection of short stories "Jehona Skenderbegiane";
    2007, a trilingual poetic drama, "Rozafa's Tears On The River Drina"
        in English, Romanian and Albanian;
    2008, a book in memory of her late husband, doctor Viktor Theohari.
    This new book it is the 16th book by Rozi.

In 2005 Rozi was honored with the "Gold Pen" Prize by the Society of Albanian-American Writers.

Rozi was awarded the "Naji Naaman's Literary Prize" in 2006 and has become an honorary member of "Masion Pour La Culture."

Four of Rozi's books are in the Library of Congress in the Washington DC.